AN UNLIKELY SAILOR

BY
J. EDWARD DAY

**The Story of a Kennedy Cabinet
Member in the World War II
Antisubmarine Navy**

**Adventures of the PC 597 and
the DE 222 (USS *Fowler*)**

mpc

McClain Printing Company
Parsons, West Virginia
1990

International Standard Book Number 0-9626033-0-9
Library of Congress Catalog Card Number 90-92974
Printed in the United States of America
Copyright © 1990 by J. Edward Day
Chevy Chase, Maryland
All Rights Reserved

CONTENTS

PREFACE

J. Edward Day was President Kennedy's postmaster general, at that time a full-fledged cabinet post. He initiated the zip code in 1963. Mr. Day is a lawyer, a farmer, a county government official, and a businessman.

Nineteen ninety is the fiftieth anniversary of the year in which it became inevitable that the United States would be a major participant in World War II. No history of the Navy's crucial role in World War II is complete without recognizing the part played by the antisubmarine fleet.

OTHER BOOKS BY J. EDWARD DAY

My Appointed Round: 929 Days as Postmaster General

Humor in Public Speaking

Descendants of Christopher Day of Bucks County, Pennsylvania

Bartholf Street (a novel)

PART I

CHAPTER ONE

I never could learn to swim. After over four years in the navy during World War II, mostly at sea, I still could barely dog paddle. Only once in all that time was I expected to swim – but that comes later.

When World War II started in Europe in the fall of 1939, I was a twenty-five-year-old lawyer practicing with a large firm in Chicago. I had decided to go to law school (Harvard) only because of a desire to get into politics, which was and is my first love. To my surprise I got very high grades at Harvard Law. As a result I was able to get a job as an associate with a large, successful firm even in those Depression days when brand new young lawyers in Chicago received the princely salary of one hundred dollars a month.

Despite my strong interest in politics I wasn't a "cause" person. But long before World War II started, I developed an intense hatred of Hitler and all that he stood for. Many of my friends were vocal isolationists, adherents of the "America First" movement which meant staying away from even the most indirect involvement in the war. The *Chicago Tribune,* which was then a super right-wing newspaper, and which, by its extreme views, had helped to turn me into a Democrat during my high school and college days in Illinois, daily attacked President Roosevelt for allegedly

3

scheming to get the United States into the war in Europe. There were lots of arguments – some of them bitter. Many people in the law office were "America Firsters." I was always an avid newspaper reader and it was frustrating to see that very few of my acquaintances seemed to realize that it was only a matter of time until the United States got into the war.

One notable exception was a forty-year-old partner in the law firm – Adlai Stevenson, later governor of Illinois and two-time presidential candidate. He and I hit it off immediately after I came to work for the firm. He was head of the Chicago branch of the Defend America by Aiding the Allies movement which was headed up nationally by William Allen White, a wise and distinguished Kansas newspaper man. In the summer of 1940, Stevenson left the firm and went to Washington as special assistant to the Secretary of the Navy, Frank Knox. Knox, and Secretary of War Stimson, were Republicans, but each was internationalist minded and had been appointed by Roosevelt in order to blunt partisanship in foreign policy. I had developed a growing feeling that I had to "do something" because of the disastrous events in Europe and my conviction that the United States was going to have to get into the war to avoid worldwide domination by Hitler.

After Germany invaded and overran Poland in September 1939 and Great Britain and France promptly declared war on Germany, nothing much happened on the Western Front for a period of eight months. This time of inactivity was referred to at the time as the "Sitzkrieg" or "Phony War" as though people were impatient for the carnage to begin.

Although Germany had been engaged in a massive military build-up for seven or eight years, Britain and France were woefully unprepared. France was complacently and foolishly relying on the elaborate and enormously costly Maginot Line of steel and concrete fortifications to defend it from attack. Part of the Maginot Line misjudgement was the assumption that Belgium and Holland, which were between France and Germany north of the Maginot Line, would be able to remain neutral. The Belgian continuation of the Maginot Line was highly vulnerable and the Dutch fortifications on the border with Germany were negligible. If France had spent all that incredible money and effort, not on a defensive series of fortresses, but on warplanes and tanks and mobile weapons, things might have been different. As it was, when the fighting began, most French artillery was pulled by horses and there were not nearly enough tanks or planes to slow down the massive and fast moving German onslaught. Germany ignored the neutrality of Holland and Belgium and on May 10, 1940, invaded both and swept across the French frontier. Just two days later, four hundred thousand allied troops were trapped at Dunkerque, Belgium but 335,000 of these were miraculously rescued and evacuated to Britain by a huge flotilla of civilian and naval craft.

The guns of Maginot Line were not capable of turning to fire against attack from the rear and the grand defense strategy of the French came to nothing. The Germans entered an undefended Paris on June 14. A week later, France and Germany signed an armistice under which the northern two-thirds of France was occupied territory and France was eliminated as a major factor in the war.

Almost at once the brutal bombing of London and environs began. Although, by incredible courage the "Battle of Britain" was ultimately won by the British, that seemed a very long shot in the summer of 1940. I watched all this with more alarm than was felt by many of my friends.

I knew of a United States naval officer training program known as the V-7 program to train deck officers to receive "D-V-G" commissions for service on naval ships. A college degree was required. The program involved spending a month on a battleship at sea and three months of intense classroom study in a naval school. In June 1940, I went over to the Naval Armory on Lake Michigan in Chicago and applied for admission to the V-7 program.

My thinking at this time was tied to a major degree to my great admiration for and confidence in the leadership of President Roosevelt. As I write this in the late 1980s, it is hard to believe that in a recent survey of high school seniors, fifty-two percent could not identify Franklin D. Roosevelt. Why Truman, effective though he was, has become a folk hero and Roosevelt has not is hard to explain.

CHAPTER TWO

"Signing Up" for the V-7 program had its problems. Each applicant was given a complete physical exam (including a test for color blindness). I passed everything in good shape until I got on the scales. I weighed in at only 130 pounds. For someone five-foot ten, that wasn't enough weight for admittance by naval standards in those pre-war days. But the naval people could see I was eager. So they told me to go someplace and cram myself with all the liquids and bananas I could hold – and then come back. After taking on all this ballast, I returned, got on the scales again, and had gotten up close enough to the minimum to get by.

The whole signing up and physical exam experience was unpleasant. The paper work and most of the physical tests were handled by career enlisted men. They didn't take too kindly to us college-types who were headed toward being "ninety day wonder"-commissioned officers. They treated us pretty much like dirt.

I found in the military (and in other of my careers, too) there are certain types who, no matter how low their place on the totem pole, take delight in tyrannizing someone who is just a little bit lower. Give a first-class seaman (who is not even a noncommissioned officer), a second-class seaman as a helper, or in naval jargon, a "striker," to help him and likely as not he will pick on and browbeat the "striker" from dawn to dusk.

Once accepted in the V-7 program, our first status was as apprentice seamen in the Naval Reserve. There is nothing lower. That part of the totem pole is barely above ground. The next step was to spend a month at sea on a battleship. That was a form of "Boot Camp" which is part of usual military procedure. The idea is to give new recruits, including officer candidates, a taste of the more rigorous part of life in the service, and to teach unquestioning response to discipline.

After a stint back at the law firm, I took a train to New York City and reported for duty on the battleship *Arkansas*. This was an antique early 1920s vessel with twelve-inch main battery guns rather than fourteen-inch on later models and sixteen-inch on battleships built during World War II.

We "V-7 types" were issued traditional enlisted men's uniforms—whites and heavier weight blues—with open necks, black neckerchiefs, and bell-bottom trousers. I was issued a hammock and assigned, with a crowd of others, to sleep in a "gun room" which was also home to a five-inch gun. The idea of the "room" was to permit the gun, when fired from a large port in the side of the ship, to recoil.

We headed for the bounding waves of the Atlantic in company with the battleship *New York*, which was of somewhat—but not much—more recent vintage than the *Arkansas*. There were also some escorting destroyers. We began to be taught about various drills such as general quarters, abandon ship, man overboard, and others. Our hammocks were slung so closely together that at night each of us pressed against the hammock occupant on either side. When it came time to rise and shine – oh so early! – we took down our hammocks, rolled them up with the blanket and pillow inside, roped and stowed them.

We headed for the United States naval base at Guantánamo Bay on the eastern end of Cuba. On the way we chipped paint and rust with hand scrapers, scrubbed decks, ate copiously, got bossed around, and listened to training talks. There was also target practice with the ship's guns – firing at a big canvas target on a barge pulled by an old four-stacker destroyer at a distance from our battleship of a mile or more. Several of us decided to watch, sitting on the open main deck practically under the 12-inch guns. With the first blast, our ears practically caved in and we retreated to a more protected vantage point. Our ship also fired anti-aircraft guns at canvas "sleeves" towed by naval planes. We novices had no part in loading or firing the guns. We learned to hold our ears.

The ships spent a couple of days in the harbor at Guantánamo. There was no big excitement there because we couldn't leave the confines of the base and had no chance to mingle with the local population. We were a long way from Havana with all its lively casinos and nightclubs.

Next we headed across the Gulf of Mexico to near the Atlantic end of the Panama Canal where we were turned loose in the civilian city. The locals, as seen on the streets and other public places, were a trashy looking lot. There were many unattractive prostitutes looking for business which meant many chances to pick up a venereal disease. The alternative was to patronize the disreputable looking bars where the regular naval crews from our battleships seemed to be familiar customers. Some of us went over to the Canal Zone to see the canal and the ships passing through. It was hot and humid even in our white summer uniforms.

Back on shipboard for the trip home, we resumed the paint and rust chipping and the deck scrubbing. The V-7 reserve apprentice seamen had another physical exam— all the usual: blood pressure, eyesight ("mine" was 20-20), color blindness, hearing, teeth (I had all mine except one wisdom tooth), pulse and hernia. I passed it all with flying colors—even weight.

We came back from the one month cruise on the battleship September 1, 1940. I got back into civilian clothes and took the train from New York City to Chicago. At this point in my life I had never flown on an airplane. Few people had.

The next step in the V-7 naval training program was to go to one of three "Ninety Day Wonder" schools and take a concentrated three-month academic course of navy subjects. Although it was fifteen months prior to the United States getting into the war, many young men were doing the same thing I was, and as a result there were no openings in any of the V-7 schools until April 1941. I went back to work at the law firm in Chicago and resumed my young bachelor life which was very much to my liking. At this point, navy-wise, I was a reserve apprentice seaman on inactive duty.

The question arose as to whether I was really qualified for the V-7 program because I had never studied trigonometry. I took a correspondence course in that difficult subject which I had about as much occasion to use in my active duty days in the navy as a knowledge of Sanskrit.

More importantly, on Valentine's Day 1941, I became engaged to a wonderful young lady who is my dear wife of forty-plus years as I write this.

CHAPTER THREE

During this six-month gap in my active involvement with the navy, I worked and socialized entirely with people in civilian life, many of whom had very little interest in the dire course of the war. In the fall of 1940, one of the senior partners in the law firm, who was an arch conservative isolationist, called me into his office to talk about politics. He was concerned that I supported the election of Roosevelt for a third term.

He was an excellent lawyer and an incredible business getter. His ability to attract and hold on to wealthy clients was a major factor in the huge financial success of the law firm. But he and I were poles apart politically. When I went to this office he poured out all the stereotyped venom of the real Roosevelt hater: "Traitor to his class," wild spender, anti-business, war monger, and all the rest. We argued for over an hour. He didn't pull rank and I gave back as much as I got. He was accustomed to coming in contact nearly exclusively with people who agreed with him ideologically. My situation was quite the reverse and I was used to political give and take. The senior partner was frustrated that he couldn't dent my conviction. His position was that it was unbelievable that a person of my ability, with the advantages I had had, could actually favor a "radical" like FDR.

Many conservative isolationists I debated with in those days ended up blaming my views on the fact that I had gone to college at the University of Chicago and to law school at Harvard. These critics thought both places had a "left-wing" influence, particularly the University of Chicago. There was nothing left-wing about me but I had long felt that if nothing were done to help the millions of unemployed, except to wait for an elusive prosperity to come around the corner, there might be no capitalism to protect. Some objective historians think we were dangerously close to revolution during the depth of the Great Depression.

The sick economy was such a preoccupation in the 1930s that a huge proportion of Americans didn't pay attention to Hitler's massive preparations for war in Europe. Hitler exploited Depression worries among the Germans to build support for his program of hate and destruction.

The wait to resume my navy training wasn't all taken up with politics and long hours at the law office. I was getting acquainted with my fiancées family and friends, and going places and doing things in a social way. It was decided that the wedding would take place right after I finished my three months of V-7 naval classroom training, even though it was expected at that time that almost immediately after the three-month course I would be heading off for duty on a navy ship.

Thanks to Roosevelt's leadership, the United States pushed ahead with efforts, short of war, to help Britain and its dominions. In the summer of 1940, large quantities of rifles, machine guns and 75-millimeter cannon were supplied to Britain. In September of 1940, Britain received fifty United States four-stacker destroyers of

World War I vintage in exchange for bases in seven British possessions. Despite the cash and carry provisions of the isolationist inspired United States Neutrality Act, deliveries of United States supplies to Britain expanded. Later the restrictive provisions of the Neutrality Act were eased by the passage by Congress of the Lend-Lease Act. Under this act, which became law on March 11, 1941, large amounts of weapons, ammunition, aircraft and other war materials were supplied, mainly to Britain and the Dominions, but also to Russia, China, and the Dutch East Indies and Latin America.

Despite the intensive bombing of London (Buckingham Palace was hit twice), despite enormous loss of shipping to Nazi submarines, and despite woeful lack of preparedness when the war started, Britain carried on the fight all over the world. In defending Egypt against the Italians and in daring victories over the Italian fleet, Britain was phenomenally successful. In trying to halt the Nazi take-over of Greece and the Balkans, Britain was disastrously unsuccessful.

In that period before the United States got into the war, many Americans believed the Allied cause was hopeless. Objectively speaking, these people were close to being right. In the summer of 1942, Churchill, the indomitable Prime Minister of Britain, told a secret session of Parliament that if, two years earlier, the Germans had crossed the English Channel with 150,000 men their invasion would have been successful.

Pessimistic attitudes in the United States about the chances of defeating the Axis powers were not changed much by the German invasion of the Soviet Union on June 22, 1941. Little was known of Russian

14

military strength. In a few months after the beginning of the invasion, German armies had reached the outskirts of Moscow and of Leningrad. The Russian government moved out of Moscow to a city further east. The Germans took 130,000 miles of Russian territory before the Russian counter offensive began to take effect. The situation on the eastern front by no means relieved the bleak prospects for the Allies.

CHAPTER FOUR

At the beginning of April, 1941, I reported for my continued V-7 training at Abbott Hall, a fairly new high-rise dormitory at the downtown campus of Northwestern University in Chicago. This building was one of three locations used by the navy for the program. It was in the area of the "near north side" where professional schools of Northwestern were located – in the neighborhood of the famous Drake Hotel and the historic Water Tower.

As a reserve midshipman I had an officer-type uniform with white shirt and tie, brass buttons, and a military cap with a visor. There were four of us in the dormitory room with two double-deck beds, four dressers and a table and chairs. We lined up in squads in the corridors and marched to the dining room, assembly hall, and classrooms. It was a little unreal – a law school graduate in a dormitory just a couple of miles from the law office where I had worked and from which, presumably I had departed for an indefinite (and probably a long) time.

There were inspections by officers assigned to run the school. A particularly unimpressive lieutenant commander named Linderman reprimanded me because my rolled up black socks were not arranged in a neat, straight row in my dresser drawer.

16

The subjects taught were navigation, gunnery, seamanship (ship handling), engineering, communications and lesser specialities. We became familiar with *The Bluejacket's Manual,* the numerous tables used in navigation and an assortment of textbooks. There were frequent tests and grades.

As the three months drew to a close, I had passed everything with flying colors. I was ready to receive my commission as a naval reserve ensign, subject to another physical examination – my third since signing up a year before. Then the incredible happened. When I took the physical, I couldn't pass the test for color blindness. The test wasn't based on recognizing the colors of lights or pieces of yarn or anything comparable to having adequate color perception in the real world. It was a so-called "Japanese" test with pages in a book depicting hundreds of little circular spots of nearly identical colors. If one's color perception was adequate, he could distinguish a large number or letter formed by spots of the same color. I couldn't make out a number or a letter on many of the pages. I had passed twice before with no question and I was sure there was a mistake of some kind. In civilian life, I had occasionally put on one dark green sock and one black sock. But with traffic lights and other practical situations I had never had difficulty.

I found out the name of a prestigious eye specialist in private practice in Chicago. I was convinced I could show that those navy medics were wrong. The doctor was anxious to help. He gave me the Japanese test. He told me I was hopelessly color-blind. The most common type of color blindness is red-green, difficulty in or inability to distinguish the two. The Japanese tests said I had it.

In my Abbott Hall class of four hundred, only three of us failed the physical. Instead of receiving an ensign's commission, each of us was released with a designation which was almost a contradiction in terms – a reserve midshipman on inactive duty. Midshipman, like cadet in the Army, was not a service rank but only a training rank. "Navy-wise," I was, as a practical matter, in limbo.

Mary Louise and I got married a few days later on July 2, 1941. After a honeymoon, I went back to work once again at the law firm. The only way I could become activated, as far as service as a reserve officer was concerned, was to be put in some kind of assignment where the color blindness would be waived. As time went on, there were discussions about me being assigned to a desk job at Great Lakes Naval Station north of Chicago as assistant to a Lieutenant Drybread (!). Nothing came of that. I was neither fish nor fowl – pretty much in a waiting status without the slightest notion what specific development I was waiting for.

On December 7, 1941, I was driving through the Chicago loop with Mary Louise and some of her family. We heard on the car radio the incredible news about the Japanese surprise attack on Pearl Harbor. At that time and practically throughout the war, very little reliable information was released about the specifics of damage to navy ships. But we all knew right away that there had been a monumental disaster. The day after the attack, President Roosevelt made his famous "Day of Infamy" speech to Congress, and war

18

on Japan was declared. Two days later we went to war with Germany and Italy.

The yellow journal tabloids were not any more responsible then, than they are now and they carried pictures showing the sunken battleship *Arizona* and other disabled vessels at Pearl Harbor. Panic set in on the West Coast due to fear of invasion. Japanese and Americans of Japanese ancestry were interned.

CHAPTER FIVE

With the United States actually at war, I was more anxious than ever to get into uniform. I talked to Adlai Stevenson at the Navy Headquarters in Washington. The navy was recruiting lawyers from civilian life to be assigned to various bureaus and headquarters divisions to back up and supplement the uniformed lawyers from the Navy Judge Advocate General's office. A brilliant New York City lawyer named Struve Hensel was the top man of this group.

I was hired to be the non-career lawyer with something called the Special Devices Section of the Bureau of Aeronautics. I was given a waiver of the color blindness and received a commission as an A-VS (Aviation – Volunteer Special) ensign instead of the D-VG (Deck – Volunteer General) commission I would have received upon completion of the V-7 program.

Our office was in a World War I "temporary" building on Constitution Avenue in Washington – within walking distance of the Lincoln Memorial. This was in an unprepossessing group of three-story concrete block buildings which housed the Navy Department headquarters. The secretary of the navy, the assistant secretaries, the chief of Naval Operations and the admirals who headed the various bureaus all had their offices there.

Mary Louise and I found an apartment in a thousand-unit spread-out complex called "Colonial Village" in Arlington, Virginia. I rode a bicycle from there across Key Bridge to my office. I bought my uniforms, winter blues and summer khakis, dress whites, a dark blue trench coat and a dark blue heavy overcoat. I had to pay for them out of my own pocket. I even had a sword, for what reason I never knew.

The mission of the Special Devices Section was to develop synthetic equipment so that men being trained as navy flyers could get part of their education through use of simulated equipment. This reduced the need to use actual planes which were in short supply.

A familiar form of a synthetic training device was the link trainer. It was a simulated airplane cockpit with instruments and controls. The trainee sat in the seat and operated the controls with the instructor looking on. The student pilot could practice the steps needed for takeoff, gaining altitude, banking, diving, landing and all the rest. The instructor could, in effect, be right there in the cockpit giving directions and correcting false moves.

Special Devices had an advanced version of this called the Visual Link. A movie in front of the student would show various views of the airspace and the ground and the trainee had to use the controls to carry out the appropriate maneuvers. There was also a version used for gunnery training. "Enemy" planes would appear on the movie screen during simulated flight and the trainee tried to aim his machine gun so as to hit the enemy. A computer-type gauge registered whether he had done so. Similar pieces of equipment can now be seen in pinball-type machines in amusement galleries. The training machines required an accurate estimate of speed, direction and distance so that the gunner would allow for the proper lead and would not use up ammunition without results.

The head of the Special Devices Section was a maverick genius named Luis (pronounced Looie) de Florez. He then had the rank of commander (the same level as a lieutenant colonel in the army or marines) and was a trained and experienced aviator. He was not "regular" navy, which for officers usually meant having graduated from Annapolis.

Luis de Florez was one of the most interesting and delightful men I have ever known. He had been an engineer in private life but had had a long connection with the navy. He hated the chain of command, red tape, bureaucracy and delay. He considered that any project he or his section was pursuing was top priority, super urgent, even frantic. He and I hit it off from the first day we met. I doubt if I have ever known a man I liked so much as Luis de Florez.

Nearly everyone in that section was a smart, gracious and superior person. Lieutenant Commander Don Hibbard was second in command. In civilian life he had been head of a Philadelphia insurance organization which provided pensions for retired Presbyterian ministers. Like Luis, he hated delay and believed in using honest shortcuts to get a project moving. His unexciting civilian job didn't seem to fit with his high powered, hard-hitting role as number two man to Commander Luis. Don was the ideal naval executive officer. In corporate life that role would be titled chief operating officer. Luis made policy. Don saw that it was carried out.

There were many other dedicated and likeable people in Special Devices. Lieutenant Commander Norman Lee was willing, charming and always ready to carry out an assignment as an all-purpose administrator. Cornelius Roosevelt was an authentic member of the Theodore Roosevelt family. He was highly intelligent, genteel, and imaginative and was involved in the engineering side of the section. In later years, he was "high up" in the CIA. There were other engineers. And there were some aviators to test the worth of the proposed synthetic training devices, in order for us to have the input of experienced navy flyers.

My main job was procurement of quantities of the devices the Special Devices Section invented, had invented, or perfected. Every procurement request had to go through various "desks" in other divisions of the Bureau of Aeronautics for approval before a contract could be finalized and the purchase could be made. To let the procurement request forms go routinely through the "system," was an invitation to unacceptable delay. The better approach was to "hand carry" anything urgent – and with Commander Luis even a requistion for more paper clips was urgent. I got to know the individuals along the approval path. It was a mixed bag, telling each one that the particular item in question was top priority and at the same time, carefully avoiding being irritating because, after all, there would no doubt be another set of papers – that I would want to ask to have put on top of the clearance pile – coming along the next day or the day thereafter.

Some of the people – civilian career people – sneered at the "urgent" designations for some of the more way-out items we wanted to purchase on an expedited basis. But not for me to reason why. I asked without embarrassment, in almost frantic tones, that the sign-off man at a desk along the way, should drop what he was doing and review the pile of papers I brought. It had never been my life's ambition but I became an expert expediter, savvy in the ways of threading through the navy paper work bureaucracy. Some of the people I dealt with were longtime, pre-war, career bureaucrats. Some procurement requests from other divisions they were processing, involved tens of millions of dollars for planes, spare parts, weapons, bombs and ammunition. They could well think of us in Special Devices as newcomer upstarts. But courtesy and appreciation on our part helped us to get over the hurdles.

CHAPTER SIX

The Training Division, of which Special Devices was a section, had more than its share of talent. The top man was Captain Arthur Radford who as the war moved on became an admiral playing an important command role in the war in the Pacific. Later he became chief of naval operations and after that chairman of the joint chiefs of staff – the highest position in the uniformed military.

Radford was a serious, formal man – not notable for a sense of humor – but a true gentleman in every way. After he left active duty in the military some years later he became identified with right-wing politics. His number two – the assistant head of the Training Division, Commander Doyle – was a forceful regular navy aviator who, a year or so later, became a rear admiral in command of a carrier task force.

One may ask why these outstanding and highly trained men were in Washington desk jobs in 1942. The reason was we didn't yet have the new warships or the new squadrons of planes. They were being rushed to completion. Training men to fly from the new carriers was all important. Top officers on carriers were and always are navy flyers.

On occasion, I was included in meetings with Radford and/or Doyle – usually involving a challenge to

Commander Luis' designation of a pet project as super urgent. Radford and Doyle liked de Florez—everybody did—but as spit and polish regular navy officers they were impatient with his unorthodox and freewheeling ways. He was not as much a thorn in the side of them as he was an annoying bumblebee. But both of these higher-ups were fair, knowledgeable, and reasonable. de Florez usually got his way.

Another notable officer in the Training Division was a lady commander named Joy Bright Hancock. Incredibly, both her first and second husbands, regular navy flyers, had been killed before the war in navy dirigible accidents. The first was on the *Shenandoah* and the second on the *Akron*. I remember as a boy in Springfield, Illinois, watching from the school yard at Butler Elementary School as the *Shenandoah* flew over our hometown. It was big excitement then. But never was a less practical military craft devised—slow, exposed, and with limited maneuverability. Big dirigibles were never used in World War II. Small blimps which dragged detection devices in the water were used in antisubmarine and anti-mine assignments. The hideous *Hindenburg* disaster before the war brought an end to the ill-fated era of giant dirigibles.

I enjoyed knowing Joy Hancock. It was unheard of to have a woman as a high ranking navy officer in 1940. She was probably the only one. The Naval Academy didn't accept women. Women military officers then were nurses. According to the book and movie *Mr. Roberts* and the TV series "M*A*S*H," military nurses were invariably glamorous and sexy. Joy Hancock was no spring chicken but she was feminine and attractive. I suppose she stayed in the Training Division for the duration of the war.

The overall head of the Bureau of Aeronautics was Rear Admiral Tower. Commander de Florez wouldn't hesitate to go to see him if necessary to get what he wanted. That was seldom necessary.

In addition to being a procurement expediter and an urgency rationalizer, I also worked on negotiating contracts for equipment and supplies. There were hoards of companies out there ready to be on the receiving end of the outpouring of government dollars. These would-be suppliers invaded our offices with persistence and regularity. Many came to sell products we didn't want. Some didn't have products – only ideas – for which the offerors would be glad to have the navy pay for production facilities. I included some of the names in a humorous poem at the time: Bassaraba, Bibitichkow, Benkenstein were some I remember.

One of the contracts to be negotiated involved a company in Connecticut. I flew up there with a Special Devices engineering specialist named Lieutenant Pomeroy. It was my first flight and not in a passenger plane but in a fighter-type, twin fuselage naval training plane called a *SNJ*.

It wasn't quite an open cockpit. There were two separated cockpits you climbed into from the top. Before you left the ground, a transparent, plastic cover slid over each cockpit. That first time in the air didn't bother me a bit, in fact, I found it exhilarating.

I flew thousands of miles during navy days without anxiety. I mention this because much later a strange thing happened. In 1955, when I was a senior officer of Prudential Insurance Company living in New Jersey, I fell and broke my back in a skiing accident. I had a complete recovery, but the falling did something to me that was irrational but real – psychologically. I developed a fear of flying.

I never got sick in the air or refused to fly but for many painful years whenever there was turbulence I had white-knuckle anxiety. There is no use telling a person who has a fear of flying that the plane isn't going to fall. You might as well tell a woman who is afraid of mice that the mouse isn't going to bite her. The whole thing is irrational. No soothing words will help. A few stiff drinks usually will – but in my series of busy legal, business, political and government careers, drinking during daytime hours was for me a "no-no."

CHAPTER SEVEN

If I were giving titles to these chapters I would call this one "Recognition." An essential of Navy Air wartime training was to teach flyers to recognize and distinguish at a glance friendly planes and enemy planes in the sky. Pictures and models were used, including brief shots on slide projector screens. We Americans had many different types of military planes and so did the British, the Japanese and the Germans. It was crucial that flyers should know the difference – and know it long before the insignia on the plane became visible.

Commander Luis conceived of an extraordinary idea. Everyone out there in the civilian hinterland wanted to "do something" to help the war effort. We would furnish the plans and patterns and ask one and all to make plane models in their home workshops to be used for recognition training.

As usual, it was no time before Luis's inspiration became a reality. By this time I had become sort of an all-purpose troubleshooter for the section. I was over-all coordinator for the volunteer model building project. I suspected that we were inviting chaos, but all of us charged ahead. We had huge amounts of patterns and instructions produced by the Government Printing Office and distributed, like income tax forms, through post offices all over the country. The program was a self-generating public relations dynamo. Newspapers, magazines and radio picked up the idea and ran with it. The instructions we distributed didn't specify that the models should be made of balsa wood. But, balsa is lightweight and easy to cut and shape. Homemade model builders commonly use balsa.

Our big error related to shipping. We should never have said to send the models to Navy Department Headquarters where the Special Devices Section was located. We couldn't use them there. They would have to be reshipped to naval air stations, such as Pensacola, Florida, where future flyers were being trained. As a result, when the thousands of containers of homemade models began arriving in a nonstoppable deluge, they literally overwhelmed the shipment receiving capacity at Navy Headquarters. The containers were stacked higher and higher, and further and further along corridors, in storerooms, and anyplace else where they could be crowded in.

But far worse was the fact that our instructions and publicity didn't drive home the fact that the models must be packaged in a highly durable way so they could stand up under very rough handling during shipment. Most parcels shipped by individuals in those days went by post office parcel post. United Parcel Service, which today carries several times more parcels than the post office, didn't accept individual shipments in those days. Their business was delivering local shipments for mass mailers such as department stores.

If, at the time I was involved in this homemade plane model project, I had known a tenth as much about post office parcel handling as I knew twenty years later as postmaster general in President Kennedy's cabinet, I could have averted some of the shipment disaster of the plane model program. In those days, and twenty years later, sorting of parcels was done by hand. The process was known as "throwing" mail. Parcel post packages mailed from rural post offices and packages of books could weigh up to as much as seventy pounds. That is *heavy*. When one of those high weight parcels was thrown or dropped into a hamper or mail sack, and landed on top of a lightly protected box containing Aunt Minnie's angel food cake, that cake is likely to acquire the shape of a very flat pie. The same is true of an inadequately wrapped plane model made of balsa or some other fragile material. Hundreds of the packages we received were broken open with the contents splintered and falling out. Even where the outer wrapping had remained more or less intact, rough treatment in shipping had often reduced the contents to kindling because these models usually were not carved or shaped out of a solid piece of material. They were assembled with replicas of wings, propellers, landing gear and fuselages. It wasn't feasible to glue the damaged ones back together. Many of the models which had been made with tender loving care were reduced, during shipment, to useless junk.

Some commercial concerns complained publicly that if we really wanted models produced with impeccable uniformity and accuracy this was no way to get them – they should be made in factories using plastics and carefully crafted molds. But many of the home-made models did arrive intact and we managed to have them shipped out to navy air training facilities. As the war went on, I saw many of these models of Japanese "Zero" fighters and other enemy planes hanging up for use in recognition training at naval bases in remote places overseas.

Commander Luis's inspiration brought on plenty of chaos. But the program was worthwhile. Luis's clout and popularity were unscathed.

CHAPTER EIGHT

I was, of course, still an ensign which was normal for a reserve officer not yet twenty-eight years old. One time as I was rushing to leave the office to take a bus downtown to lunch, I accidentally took from a hanger and put on, a coat belonging to one of our lieutenant commanders with the shoulder boards and two and a half stripes. That rank is the same as a major in the other services. The coat fit and I didn't realize my mistake. When I got out to the bus stop on Constitution Avenue, the various naval officers standing there stared at me with curiosity because I looked too young to be a lieutenant commander. The stares were so noticeable that I woke up to what I had done and went back to change coats.

Naval officers as a group, whether regular or reserve, were inclined to be rank conscious. This was much less so among the uniformed personnel in the Special Devices Section. Commander Luis wanted results and he delegated responsibility and authority regardless of rank. Don Hibbard felt the same way. As a result, I, for example, had men three officer ranks above me, working under my general supervision. It was made easier for them by the fact that some of them, purely because they were older, had been taken in at higher ranks directly from civilian life.

Most of the Special Devices officers had had no navy training whatever. This was even true of some of the aviators. This informal approach was a natural consequence of the fact that Commander Luis expected no formality or reverence toward himself. He was very much in charge but he didn't have to rely on the stripes on his uniform to have everyone realize it.

His quixotic tolerance toward informality is illustrated by an incident I remember that took place at one of the fairly frequent parties Special Devices people, including clerks and secretaries, took part in. I have mentioned link trainers, the best known of synthetic training devices for training of flyers. We also had "Visual Links" which had a motion picture projector and curved screen attached in front of the cockpit so that sky, landscape, landing strips and other planes were seen in various angles, positions and altitudes depending on the trainee's operation of the controls.

In advance of one of our parties, which were not of a teetotaler variety, I drew a cariacature of Luis with his bald head, waxed mustache and short, muscular build. Underneath I put the following doggerel:

> "Here you see Commander Luis,
> King of all devices screwey,
> To Japs he'd be an awful jinx,
> If wars were fought in Visual Links."

I read this off before the assembled group and Luis liked it thoroughly. His laugh was infectious.

During this time, Mary Louise and I saw Adlai Stevenson, who continued as special assistant to Secretary of Navy Knox and never donned a uniform. He

34

would have had to be a captain (same level as a "chicken colonel" in the other services) to be aide to the secretary. Adlai's wife, who divorced him shortly after he became governor of Illinois in 1949, was seldom in Washington. Adlai was under great pressure and also was away a great deal, traveling with or for the secretary. But when he was in town he enjoyed a chance to have dinner with friends and we joined him then. His true anecdotes were superlative.

There was one about a visit to Secretary Knox by a group of government leaders from China. Knox was an authentic Bull Mooser from the Theodore Roosevelt days. He was intelligent and hardworking but inclined on occasion to be blustering and tactless. The Chinese delegation was concerned about indications that the United States was going to give first priority, in its war effort, to defeating Hitler and then concentrating on the defeat of Japan. This was in fact true because with Britain fighting on, we had a base of operations close to Germany, but, at that time, none close to Japan. China was largely crushed under a brutal occupation by Japanese forces and the Chinese delegation wanted the Pacific war to have first priority. Knox reassured the China group that there would be a strong United States effort in the Pacific, that China would not be forgotten, and that fears of a second priority United States policy were groundless. As the Chinese delegation was leaving his office, Knox saw them out the door and, with his characteristic backslapping heartiness, said to them: "Don't worry. We'll get those yellow bellied bastards."

Another Stevenson anecdote had to do with the elegant, Oxford-educated Chinese Ambassador to the

United States, Wellington Koo. Koo was to speak at a Washington luncheon meeting. By chance, an unsophisticated American businessman of the red-neck type was seated next to him. The American was at a loss as to how to start a conversation with a Chinese person. Finally after the first course was served the American turned to Koo and asked: "Likee soup?" Koo nodded and said nothing. Later he delivered an eloquent and informative speech in his usual perfect English. When he sat down and the applause had subsided he turned to the American and, with a straight face, said: "Likee speech?"

On one of his trips with Knox, Stevenson heard about an American sailor who was being court-martialed for making a sexual assault on a male native of a South Pacific island where the navy had set up a base. The sailor had said in his defense: "I was hiding in a bush hoping to have some sex with a native girl. I saw one coming along wearing a tight, bright colored, flowered dress. I pulled the native into the bush with me. I was so surprised when I found out it was a boy I almost let him go."

CHAPTER NINE

In the fall of 1942, Commander Luis arranged for me to receive a "spot promotion." This advanced me to Lieutenant j.g. The j.g. stood for "junior grade" and the rank was the same as first lieutenant in the other services. A spot promotion was one that was effective only as long as the officer stayed in the same assignment. This was the turning point in my naval career.

In order to qualify for the promotion I had to pass another physical examination. I went over to the headquarters of the Navy's Bureau of Medicine and Surgery on a hill off of 23rd Street. I went through the various tests. When I got to the color blindness part and the charts of closely similar shades of colored dots I was trying hard but failing as before.

By a weird chance a regular navy four-striper (captain) medical officer came by. He looked at my efforts and asked me if I was color-blind. I told him that for practical purposes I wasn't – that I could see objects and lights and their colors at a great distance, and that I wanted sea duty. His answer: "We don't use the colored light test anymore but come on in to this room and I will let you try it."

It was, in fact, a realistic test with colored lights and I passed it – I will avoid saying with flying colors – but without difficulty. To my amazement he wrote on my yellow medical record folder "This man is never to be questioned again on color blindness – signed – Captain – – – U.S.N. Bureau of Medicine and Surgery." This was a bombshell.

I told Commander Luis and Don Hibbard what had happened and what I planned to do. They didn't want me to leave Special Devices, but they knew I wanted sea duty and they assured me they would not only not stand in the way but they would, instead, help.

The appropriate papers were prepared and submitted to the Bureau of Navigation (later the Bureau of Personnel) requesting that the D-VG (deck volunteer general) classification for which I had been trained at Abbott Hall be assigned in place of the A-VS (aviation volunteer special) classification with which I was serving in the Bureau of Aeronautics on a waiver. I felt that a person with my strongly independent temperament would be better off serving on a smaller ship rather than on one with a complement of one or two thousand men and a hundred or more officers. The place to be prepared for service on a small ship was the Submarine Chaser Training Center (SCTC) at Miami, Florida. I included an application to go there. My requests were granted.

There was a wait to get into SCTC and I stayed on and kept busy for two months at Special Devices. What was going on on the war fronts during this year of 1942 while I worked for Commander Luis? Early in the year, Britain surrendered Singapore to the Japanese. Some experts say Singapore was indefensible. Others say the disaster there was caused by the Maginot Line blunder all over again; the defenses were set up to fend off an attack from the south, but the Japanese came down behind the defenses from the north. In April, the American and Filipino forces surrendered the Philippines to the Japanese. There was the humiliating Bataan Death March of starving, injured and mistreated American prisoners of war. General Douglas MacArthur moved to a new headquarters at Brisbane on the east coast of Australia.

There were important battles at sea in the Pacific: the Battle of the Java Sea (a loss for the Allies), the four-day Battle of the Coral Sea (with heavy losses of ships and planes on both sides and no clear victory for either) and the Battle of Midway, probably the turning point in the war in the Pacific. In successfully defending Midway, the Americans sank all four of the Japanese heavy carriers and the Japanese lost most of their navy's best trained pilots.

China formally became one of the Allies with Chiang Kai-shek in command and United States General Joseph W. Stilwell as chief of staff. The land war in Burma was a failure for the Allies. But the Allies had their first successes of the Pacific war during the summer and fall of 1942. In a series of engagements, the Japanese were driven out of Guadalcanal and other islands in the central Solomon Islands where they had planned to construct an air base. Numerous heavy warships were lost by each side as though they were pawns in a chess game. Also in late 1942, the United States began the successful expulsion of Japanese from the Aleutian Islands in Alaska.

Somehow activity in the Pacific seemed more important to home-front navy observers of the war, perhaps because of an unconscious feeling that the navy's disastrous losses at Pearl Harbor must be avenged. But action against the Germans in Russia and Africa in 1942 was equally crucial and perhaps even more decisive in the overall war effort. Hitler's forces were bogged down by the Russian winter in 1941-42. But by spring, the Germans resumed their giant offensive against the Soviets. Fortunately, incredible Russian resistance stopped the Germans at Stalingrad. A 1,000-day siege of Leningrad went on with the German encirclement so tight that neither reinforcements nor supplies could reach the city. During the siege, one million people died of starvation including the man in charge of bread rationing.

In late 1942, the Allies invaded northwest Africa, the beginning of eliminating the Germans from that theatre of operations. In the Atlantic, German U-boats in 1942 sank more than six million tons of shipping. It was the middle of the year before the Allies introduced the convoy system. It was partially effective but the Germans were turning out large numbers of new submarines and began using U-tankers, large converted U-boats equipped to supply fuel, torpedoes and supplies to U-boats operating in remote waters.

British bombing of German cities began in early 1942 and continued relentlessly despite enormous losses of planes and crews. We, in Special Devices, followed all these widely scattered and monumental activities as best we could. We, of course, did not know the strategy or the significance of much that was going on. Incredible as it seems, the American public and most military personnel at all but the highest levels, did not know specifically how bad the losses had been in the Pearl Harbor attack on December 7, 1941. There were articles about the disaster in tabloids and photographs said to be from Japanese sources, but we didn't know whether they were reliable. Only much later did we learn authoritatively that all eight United States battleships at Pearl Harbor were hit. Five were sunk and another heavily damaged. Eleven other ships were sunk or crippled and 140 planes were destroyed.

Only late in the war did I fully realize how fortunate it was that my period of enforced desk duty in Washington was spent with such stimulating people as Commander Luis attached to Special Devices. I did not regret telling all these people good-bye, much as I liked and admired them. I had been bucking for sea duty from the beginning and now that phase of my navy life was about to begin.

CHAPTER TEN

At the end of 1942, Mary Louise and I gave up our apartment in Colonial Village in Arlington, Virginia, sent our furniture and furnishings to Chicago for storage, and headed for Miami by train. A derailment caused us to be stopped dead for twenty-four hours in Americus, Georgia.

In Miami, we soon found a furnished apartment at an exhorbitant price typical of the wartime "rip offs" of military people by greedy civilians. The SCTC was on a large pier which jutted out into Biscayne Bay, the body of water between Miami and Miami Beach. The many high-rise hotels across in Miami Beach had been taken over by the Air Force as dormitories for huge classes of officer candidates who were being trained for non-flying, administrative duties. The SCTC contingent were already officers, were not housed together, and were scattered in apartments and rooms of various sorts around the area.

The classwork was sort of a graduate course in what I had been taught at Abbott Hall in Chicago with concentration on detecting and destroying enemy submarines. There were four main categories of navy antisubmarine vessels. The largest were DEs, standing for destroyer escorts, which were 350 feet long and had diesel or steam power. They were much slower versions of destroyers and were being mass produced to operate as escorts for convoys in the Atlantic or other waters where the seas could be too rough for smaller antisubmarine craft. The second category was PCs, standing for patrol craft, which were 176 feet long, with diesel engines and three-inch guns. Next came SCs, standing for submarine chasers. They were 110 feet long with diesel engines and one three-inch gun. The fourth category consisted of converted private yachts which were of various lengths, some quite slow and unimpressive looking. Since the great majority of all of these craft had diesel engines, our training in engineering at SCTC was more meaningful than the broad-brush approach at Abbott Hall where the graduates could be assigned to anything from battleships to reefers (refrigerated supply ships).

The course work at SCTC was highly concentrated and demanding with much homework. At least we didn't have to do a lot of marching and drilling or worry about keeping our rolled up socks in straight rows in our dresser drawers.

Since my promotion to lieutenant j.g. at Special Devices had been on a "spot" basis, I received word soon after arriving at SCTC that I was an ensign again. It was disappointing to have to take the half stripe off of all my uniforms, but the vigilant friendship and magic of Commander de Florez was still at work. I soon received word that I had been promoted back to j.g. on a regular basis. Even then, I was beginning to be more interested in my navy rank. That is because, despite some Allied successes, I, and many of my friends couldn't see how there was ever going to be an end to the two wars we were involved in. I began to think of military service as a career for an extended period. Being an ambitious type I wanted to move onward and upward. I had no way to know big brains were working on developing an atom bomb. I had never heard of such a possible weapon. Only long after the war did I learn that Albert Einstein had told President Roosevelt before the United States got into the war that it might well be possible to develop an atomic bomb.

CHAPTER ELEVEN

When our class finished the course at SCTC, each of us received our orders from the Bureau of Navigation in Washington. I was assigned as executive officer, i.e., the second highest officer, on *PC-597*. The orders didn't say specifically where the ship was, but I knew it was not just getting ready to become operational and that it was somewhere in the Pacific because my orders said to go to San Diego, California, and await transportation. The ticket for the train trip was arranged by the navy people in Miami.

Mary Louise went back to Winnetka, Illinois, a suburb north of Chicago, to stay with her parents. She was pregnant but the due date was several months away.

I put up in a hotel in San Diego for a few days and then, pursuant to instructions, boarded a large navy transport, which had been a passenger liner called the *Columbia* before the war, for transit to Honolulu. The trip was made on the assumption that we might be attacked at anytime, particularly in the first light of morning, by Japanese submarines. The ship was blacked out at night. Before sunup all the passengers, made up of both navy officers and enlisted men, lined up in their life jackets on the open deck at their abandon-ship stations near the lifeboats to which each was assigned. We stayed there a couple of hours each morning until the most likely time for a submarine attack had passed.

We were fast enough that we didn't have a warship escort. Speed was important for transports. The *Queen Mary*, which was very fast, made dozens of trips during the war back and forth across the Atlantic, carrying ten thousand troops at a time, with no escort – because no submarine could have kept up with her.

An aside about that great British ship – she was built as a passenger liner by the Cunard Line. Cunard ships had customarily been given names ending with "ia" – the *Lusitania*, the *Maurtania*, the *Aquitania*, etc. The Cunard management wanted to name this largest ship ever built after Queen Victoria. At that time the King of Britain was Queen Victoria's grandson, George V, whose wife was Queen Mary. As a matter of courtesy the top officials at Cunard went to see the king. They described the great new ship and said they wanted to name her "after the greatest Queen England has ever had." King George immediately replied: "Queen Mary will be very pleased." That is how the ship got her name. Today she is landlocked at Long Beach, California, as a hotel, convention center and sightseeing attraction.

As passengers on the transport to Honolulu, we had no duties. We couldn't go to "officers' country," which is where the officers running the ship had their quarters, or to the wardroom where they had their meals and spent off-duty time. We passengers spent our time eating (cafeteria-style in a large dining room), sleeping, playing cards and watching movies. Most of us, unless it was someone returning to previous assignment on a base or ship, didn't know

46

whether we would be finishing our transportation in Hawaii or whether we would be moving further on to some other location.

It was 2,100 miles from San Diego to Honolulu and it took us five days to get there. The Pacific got its name because it is usually fairly calm. We had no really rough weather on our trip across. Nonetheless, some of the passengers were seasick. Seasickness is a scourge of the surface navy for those who are susceptible to it. Fortunately for me, as I found out later, if it was smooth the first ten or twelve hours after leaving port, and I could get my sea legs, I didn't get seasick no matter how rough it got.

We arrived in Honolulu and there was the usual Hawaiian welcoming hoopla of hula girls, music and flowered leis. I went by navy bus to an anchorage area which was part of Pearl Harbor and reported to *PC-597*.

CHAPTER TWELVE

PC-597 hadn't been told they were getting a new executive officer. They already had one and he had received no indication that he was being transferred. I was about as welcome as a skunk at a lawn picnic. My friendly ways didn't cut any ice.

The ship had four officers before I arrived and sixty enlisted men. They had all been a part of putting the ship in commission eight months before, after it was built in Bremerton, Washington.

For reasons that will be clear later, I won't use the actual names of these four original officers. The commanding officer, called the captain, was an Ivy League-type, a lieutenant (same rank as an army or marine or air force captain) named Lance Chapin. He was a little older than I, an eastern establishment type. The executive officer was a j.g., named John Maddox. He was quite a bit older than any of the rest of us – in his mid-forties. In private life, he had been a writer of detective mysteries and he was indeed highly literate and sophisticated. The third of the four officers was an ensign named Keith Ryan, who had worked for a large correspondence school. He was as Irish as his name: auburn hair, reddish, freckled complexion. He was quite a handsome fellow. I soon learned that his top motivation was to have his sea duty assignment terminated and to be assigned to shore duty. He was nominally the communications officer for the ship but he paid very little attention to that or anything else that required work. The fourth of the officers was Bob Boren, another ensign, in his early twenties. He was a brash, bouncy, overly self-confident person who had the title of gunnery officer. He likewise had no intention of exerting himself any more than was absolutely necessary.

My situation as the new arrival who had been told he was going to be executive officer, was that I was a fifth wheel as far as the other officers were concerned. A PC was designed for four officers. There were two officers' cabins with an upper and lower bunk and two sets of metal drawers and two small closets in each. However, PCs often did have five officers. This one never had, until now. It wasn't feasible at this point for me to suggest or insist that one of the ensigns should move to provide me with proper quarters. Chapin wouldn't have backed me up. There was only my word for it that I was supposed to be executive officer. My orders didn't say anything about that – I had only been told orally at SCTC in Miami. I had no clout – and no bunk.

Without consulting me, Chapin and Maddox, who were thick as thieves, decided I should sleep on a cot out in the open on the upper deck. I was to have a tarpaulin to pull over me when it rained. I was burned up but there was no use making an issue of the situation.

There was a hierarchy of naval officers in offices next to the area where the submarine chasers were tied up, who were in charge of the PCs and SCs. PCs and SCs didn't operate in squadrons where the captain of one ship was in charge of a group of ships. We got no orders from other ships – only direct from our shore headquarters. The top man of our Pearl Harbor shore headquarters was a four-striper captain named Barnett. He was a "mustang" which meant he had come up from the ranks. Barnett was gruff and tough, of the same unimpressive ilk as the officer at Abbott Hall who had bawled me out for not having my rolled-up socks in a straight row in the dresser drawer. If I had complained to Barnett or one of his staff officers about my assignment to a cot on the deck, something might have been done. But I would have further increased the antagonism which had arisen on *PC-597* merely because of my unwelcome arrival.

Theoretically, my sleeping arrangement could have caused me embarrassment with the crew – particularly with the chief petty officers (like top sergeants) who kept the show on the road on a small ship like ours. But, I soon learned that Chapin was not liked or respected by most of the crew. They probably concluded, with the cynical attitude of enlisted men toward the military establishment in general, that the brass had made one of their usual blunders and that there had been some foul up in my assignment.

There were various departments even on that small ship: navigation, deck, engineering, communications, gunnery and supply. It wasn't clear at first where I was going to fit. But, I did come in handy right from the start because I could help to stand watches. Watches at sea were each four hours long starting at midnight, then 4:00 a.m., 8:00 a.m., noon, 4:00 p.m., and 8:00 p.m. Watches were divided into half hour periods, marked by a rap on the ship's bell, so the end of a watch was eight bells. It was up to the captain whether he stood watches and Chapin never did. But with four, instead of three other officers, each one's frequency of watches at sea was reduced. This had an added advantage. With four officers not on watch, we could play bridge and each of us liked that game and played often and reasonably well.

There were some outstanding chief petty officers on the ship. The chief quartermaster, a man in his forties named Yoemans (real name), knew celestial navigation. That involved determining the location of the ship by use of a sextant to measure the degree of angle of a particular star or planet above the horizon. This information was then compared with elaborate navigational tables in books which were kept updated by supplements received in the mail.

How the mariners of old kept track of their locations with no charts (detailed maps of navigable waters) and no navigational tables, is a mystery. I suppose one answer is that they didn't. The *Mayflower* headed out from Plymouth, England in 1620, intending to sail to Virginia. They ended up in what is now Massachusetts. If they had made it to Virginia there wouldn't have been any Mayflower Society or proud talk about *Mayflower* descendants. Because in 1620, the Pilgrims would have found quite a few English already settled in the Jamestown, Virginia area. In fact, by 1620, some settlers who were headed for Jamestown ended up by accident on the island of Bermuda — only seven hundred miles from the North American coast. In 1620, these Bermuda settlers formed a parliament, the first one in the world outside of London.

The group which landed at Plymouth Rock have had such good public relations buildup that many people think these Pilgrims were the first English to settle in North America. I don't know why the Jamestown settlers missed out on the public relations hype. As an aside, those who revel in their *Mayflower* ancestry overlook the fact that half the passengers on that ship were indentured servants – pretty close to slaves.

But . . . back to navigation. There are several other methods besides measuring the angles of celestial bodies. "Dead reckoning" involves keeping close track of the speed (using knowledge of distance covered at different settings of the engines) and direction (derived from the compass). The "standard speed" on a PC was 15 knots. A knot is one nautical mile per hour. A nautical mile is one and one-sixth regular miles. Dead reckoning had many chances for inaccuracies such as effect of wind or current on speed. Every time speed or direction is changed while a ship is underway, that change and the time it is made must be noted in the ship's log. So location is determined, for example, by calculating 2 hours at 15 knots at compass reading 259 degrees; one-half hour at 10 knots, same direction; 3 hours at 15 knots at 230 degrees.

In modern-day navigation there are also radio direction finders which show by radio directions from given points where the transmission originates. When two or more of these direction lines are marked on the ship's chart for the area, an exact location is derived. We didn't have a radio direction finder on our ship. There was, however, other equipment which sometimes helped with navigation. Our fathometer told the depth of water under us. Our charts showed depths at all locations at sea. If the depth on the fathometer, and particularly changing depths, matched up with those at a particular area on the chart it gave some indication of where we were. When we were within sight of shore we could take bearings (compass directions) of navigational aids such as lighthouses or buoys, and of natural feaures such as Diamond Head east of Pearl Harbor. Dead reckoning, with all its faults, had to be used in bad weather when no heavenly bodies could be seen. We used it all the time at sea and checked our locations with celestial navigation when we could. There wasn't anything comparable to air traffic control stations on shore which would try to keep track of where various friendly ships were, or should have been located.

There were huge metal submarine nets across the entrance to Pearl Harbor, a very important precaution. During the war, three Japanese mini-submarines managed to get under the nets into the huge harbor at Sydney, Australia. One was sunk by an American warship, one was captured, and the third was never accounted for. This meant that the nets would not give "sure-fire" protection. Part of our PC's assignment was to patrol with our sound gear back and forth on an arc outside the harbor. Many ships of all sizes were inside the harbor – hopefully more on the alert than when command blundering made possible the December 7, 1941, debacle.

We patrolled the harbor area several days and nights at a time. Our shore command center would then tell us to come back into the harbor, refuel, reprovision and give the ships company some liberty. On frequent occasions our ship was ordered out to escort a merchant ship, or tanker, into Pearl Harbor. We would usually go out about two hundred miles, rendezvous with a ship coming from stateside, and escort it in, by "steaming" (applied even to diesel-powered ships) in front of it using our sound gear. The sound gear used underwater the same technique that was used for radar in the open. The sonar sound beams from our transmitter under the ship would sweep a large area and if a beam hit something solid and bounced back it just might be a submarine. More likely it was an underwater reef, a sunken wreck, a school of fish or a whale. There were many false alarms.

The thinking was that the enemy submarine danger greatly increased close to land where there was a concentration of shipping. As a result we also received frequent assignments to escort merchant ships to ports on other Hawaiian islands. On the "big island" of Hawaii (the one with the volcanoes, the hot bubbling lava springs and the black sand beach), there were two ports, Hilo and the Parker Ranch. The Parker Ranch was, after the King Ranch in Texas, the second largest piece of real estate under one private ownership in the United States. Ships we escorted brought supplies into both of those ports. Parker Ranch seemed more like the old west than part of a tropical island. There were thousands of head of cattle and real cowboys. We came ashore, and since no major navy ships called there, we were given a royal welcome.

On one of our assignments we went to Johnson Island which was seven hundred miles west of Honolulu but still a part of the Territory of Hawaii (Hawaii

54

didn't become a state until 1958). Johnson Island was an atoll which was useful only as a naval air base. Our PC anchored there a couple of days to wait for the supply ship to unload so that we could escort it back. The Chief Boatwain's mate and two other enlisted men and I, borrowed an oversized rowboat with an outboard and went fishing. We caught a lot of good fish – snapper and grouper. The fish in the boat attracted huge flocks of sea gulls which flew down almost close enough to touch. At one point I whipped my fishing rod at the birds to drive them off. My fishhook caught and stayed in the beak of a large gull. It carried my line out a couple of hundred feet into the air. The whole flock followed. Then when I reeled in my line and brought the bird down right above the boat, the flock came down *en masse*. I had control of a big flock of gulls and could bring them in close or let them fly some distance out. It was a ludicrous sight. I eventually brought the hooked bird down to the boat, freed it, and the flock went on their way.

Fishing was a big thing in our life at sea. Enlisted men who were not on duty often had fishing lines trailing from the fantail (stern) of the ship when we were underway. If they caught something big, they yelled up to the bridge and the ship was stopped long enough to permit the fish to be brought abroad. Usually it was a shark which was clubbed to death, cleaned and sent to the galley. Shark meat isn't bad eating.

CHAPTER THIRTEEN

A couple of months after I first reported to the *PC-597*, John Maddox, the executive officer, received orders to report back to the mainland for further duty. I became officially the executive officer and acquired a shared officer's cabin and a bunk. Since the two ensigns weren't interested in work, and I was restless and seeking authority, I gradually took over all of the officer assignments except command and gunnery. Besides being executive officer, I became, and continued to be for about a year, engineering officer, communications officer and supply officer. One of the lazy ensigns had the silly title of morale officer. Keith Ryan spent as much time as possible sitting out in the bright sun clad in bathing shorts hoping that his Irish skin would become seriously blistered and he would receive, courtesy of some navy doctor, orders to shore duty. Captain Lance Chapin, Chief Quartermaster Yoemans and I handled navigation between the three of us.

As supply officer, I was also commissary officer, in charge of the provisions and the cooks. Our cooks for the crew were not trained as such. If one of them had flipped hamburgers in a diner he was a qualified expert. The mess hall was also the bunk room for most of the crew and also their recreation room where they played cards and wrote letters. The crew's food wasn't bad and there was lots of it. The big lack was ice cream. A ship our size lacked four important items: an ice cream-making machine, a movie projector, a small boat that could be carried aboard and used to go ashore when we were anchored out, and equipment to make an adequate supply of fresh water. A salt-water shower leaves you sticky.

There was lots of eating between meals such as before going on a midnight or 4 a.m. watch. The navy had in ample supply the things that were being rationed at home such as butter and red meat. I discovered that many enlisted men, particularly those who had been brought up on farms, thought that lamb wasn't fit to eat—anymore than dog or donkey. We were issued lots of lamb and sometimes a leg of lamb was surreptitiously thrown overboard.

The officers ate like kings. In World War II the military services were segregated. There were no blacks in the deck crew or the engineering crew. Finally, President Truman ended segregation in the armed forces—after World War II. We had two blacks on board. Their sole job was to cook for and wait on the officers. By good luck, one of our officer's stewards, a man named Poydras, had been a cook in a New Orleans restaurant. He delighted in cooking up delicacies: creole dishes, rich pies and pasteries and other fattening items. In June, 1940, I had had to stuff myself with bananas to meet the weight requirement for acceptance by the navy. On shipboard I soon gained twenty-five pounds. I had never lived an outdoor life before. The salt air increased my already voracious appetite. Also, as I said, we did much eating between meals. It was something to do. For many the only dissipation was coffee drinking. In the engine room and in the galley there were always a pot of coffee on a hot plate. Some crew members drank as much as thirty cups of coffee a day. How they ever slept I don't understand—but they did. They craved any kind of stimulant because for many long, boring days they couldn't get liquor—even beer. They drank anything that had alcohol in it. Shaving lotion was a favorite. After a few swigs of that a man would be helplessly passed out on the deck. It's difficult to keep people from drinking non-beverage liquids if they are determined to do so.

I once asked a capable petty officer, a first class gunner's mate, after one of these bouts whether drinking shaving lotion made him feel better. He said, no, it didn't, but it made him feel "different." The monotony was grueling for many of these men who had very limited intellectual resources—if any. Sex and booze were their main interests. One advantage of living in close quarters with uneducated, uninspired, sometimes really dumb people, was that you had a chance to learn to get along with nearly everybody.

That was highlighted by the four-hour watches on the bridge. The officer of the deck did not touch the wheel or the speed controls. There was a seaman or petty officer at the wheel, another at the engine room telegraph, which was the name for the speed controls. There was a quartermaster who watched the charts and made entries in the log. There was a sonar man manning the sound gear, a radioman and lookouts.

At night, we were completely blacked out. In order to work at charts it was necessary to go behind a heavy curtain where there was light over the chart table. The blackout had an advantage. Your eyes became accustomed to the dark and it is amazing what you can see even on a moonless night when your eyes become adjusted. A careful officer of the deck did not rely on the lookouts to spot another ship that might be underway in the vicinity. The officer used his binoculars to scan the horizon.

Some enlisted men talked endlessly when they were on the bridge on watch. The context of the conversation was indescribedly boring. It usually had to do with exaggerated accounts of sexual acts. One learned all the sordid details of operation of an assembly line style of brothel. The men weren't even assigned to a room but to a cubicle with a cot and a curtain. The woman went from cubicle to cubicle with only a few minutes in each. If the man wasn't ready she didn't wait around but went on to the next. There was no time for foreplay, no privacy, only a quick encounter with a female who functioned much like a machine – or perhaps more like an animal. We heard these stories night after night on the bridge. They became more exaggerated and embellished as the men sought to convince themselves and the others that they had had exciting carnal adventures.

The worst part was when the ship was in port – particularly a new port – and the men had liberty. Usually half the crew and all but one officer went ashore. For many of the enlisted men the sole object seemed to be to get as drunk as possible – falling-down drunk, sick drunk, unconscious drunk, sometimes mean drunk. Many of them were hauled back to the ship in trucks by the locally-based shore patrol.

The scenes in *Mister Roberts* of hoisting a cargo net full of passed out crew members back aboard the ship were entirely accurate.

Men who were mild mannered when sober sometimes went wild from too much alcohol. At one port a ship's cook began chasing anyone he could find with a large butcher knife. I was officer of the deck that particular night – the only officer aboard. The officer of the deck wore sidearms but it wasn't in the cards to do any shooting or even to take the .45 out of the holster. By some miracle I got that raving, out of control man to give up his knife and to start sleeping it off in his bunk. Some of those staggering back or being hauled back to the ship had been in brawls and had cuts and black eyes and bloody noses.

When we officers went ashore for a night's liberty it was usually to officers' clubs. It was no pleasure to be around in the streets of a port because the whole place was rigidly blacked out and there was no respect for rank in the jostling mob.

There was a cynical joke during the war about a violent battle by American forces to recapture a remote island that had been occupied by the Japanese. When the carnage was finally over and the Americans managed to wade ashore the very first thing that was done was to set up an officers' club!

There was a certain amount of truth in that. Under regulations, promulgated by Secretary of Navy Josephus Daniels during World War I, no liquor was permitted on navy ships. As one and all know now from the television series M*A*S*H, medical alcohol mixed with pineapple juice or even taken straight as a close imitation of a martini wasn't a bad drink. But it was hard to get hold of, and only the officers sometimes had it. In remote locations during World War II, there was discrimination in the hard liquor department. At officers' clubs there was hard liquor and at enlisted men's clubs or canteens there was only beer and wine. Of course, some people can get hopelessly inebriated just on beer. And since rum and coke or bourbon and coke were the favorite drinks in officers' clubs, the aftereffects of a large quantity of those sweet drinks were often sickening.

CHAPTER FOURTEEN

Back to what was happening in the big picture of World War II in 1943. The situation on all major fronts in that year has caused historians to call it "The Year of Preparations." The Allies were not yet prepared for the cross-channel invasion into France but were building up large offensive strength. During the year the Russians cleared most of the Germans from their soil. The effect of the Nazi mentality of rule or ruin was damaging to German military operations. They held on to exposed positions to the bitter end rather than following a principle of elastic defense in depth. The Germans were sacrificing crack troops in trying to hold on to captured territory which could not be held.

In 1943, the Mediterranean furnished what seemed at the time to be the most significant developments. The Axis armies in Tunisia were destroyed and the Allies moved up through Sicily and Sardinia, invaded Italy, and brought on the fall of the loathsome Mussolini and the surrender of the Italian government and of the Italian fleet. There was a "book" at the time with the title emblazoned on the front cover: "Great Italian War Heroes." All the pages inside were blank.

We on the *PC-597* and on other ships in our area had our attention riveted much more on developments in the Pacific. The actions of that year seemed relatively small scale in the Solomons and New Guinea. Attu and Kodiak in the Aleutians were recovered from the Japanese. Toward the end of the year, the island of Tarawa in the west central Pacific was taken by the Americans with heavy casualties. But to observers such as we were on our ship, with no special knowledge of grand strategy, the progress in the Pacific seemed to be agonizingly slow. Even with the successes in Russia and the Mediterranean and the reduction of the submarine threat in the Atlantic and the beginning of heavy allied air raids over Germany, the Germans talked of "Fortress Europe" meaning they meant to hold on forever. In the Pacific the retaking of the Philippines and of the Southeast Asia mainland seemed far, far away. We knew nothing of the Manhattan Project to try to perfect an atomic bomb. The thought of invading the Japanese main islands themselves seem to involve an effort and a loss of American lives that was too horrendous to contemplate.

It seemed the war would go on at least another five years. A slogan developed in the Pacific navy: "Golden Gate in '48." All of this had an impact on my own thinking. The thought went through my mind of becoming a career naval officer rather than considering that long time in uniform merely an interruption of my civilian career as a lawyer. Advancement in the navy became a definite and crucial goal. I had lost a rank by virtue of failing to get a commission when I finished Abbott Hall. I became a full lieutenant in late 1943 – but if it hadn't been for the color blindness delay I would have become, instead, a lieutenant commander, (same as an

63

army major). As a lieutenant commander I would have been a commanding officer of a larger antisubmarine warfare vessel.

As it was, the system was that a commanding officer of a PC or an SC served for a year or a year and a half and then was moved on for further training and service on a larger ship. Then, with few exceptions, the PC or SC executive officer moved up to command. For an executive officer it was essential that his captain should be well regarded by higher authority so that the captain would move onward and upward and make way.

I wasn't on the *PC-597* very long before I began to realize something important was very wrong. Our commanding officer, Mr. Chapin, for some reason was in bad with our next level of command, Captain Barnett and his staff at the Submarine Chaser Command Center. When coming alongside a dock or when dropping anchor the captain of a ship takes over the bridge and is in charge of the ship handling. Chapin didn't always do a smart, seamanlike job of handling the ship. Bringing it alongside a dock wasn't all that difficult with the smooth water of a harbor and twin propellers which gave increased maneuverability. On one occasion, Chapin banged the ship against the dock and knocked down all the metal "stanchions" or supports for the light cables which were the "railing" around the main deck. On another occasion we had engine trouble and our excellent chief motor machinist mate, a man named Hayes, said we couldn't fix the trouble unless we had a particular tool which we weren't carrying on board. There was another submarine chaser patroling in the distance. We signaled and found they had the needed tool. The sea was not rough and we approached to borrow the needed item – and in the process collided with the other ship – by no means a mere nudge. When we had made the repairs and were ready to come up to the other ship again, they told us to keep our distance and threw over a long line to which the tool was tied and pulled back manually to their deck. It was like certain people who never learn how to park a car in limited space at a curb.

But these weren't world shaking incidents – probably not too unusual. Chapin also had discipline problems with the crew. The navy, of course, has court martials and a curtailed version called summary court martials. But they couldn't be used on board a small ship such as ours. If the offense was sufficiently serious to require one, such as desertion, or stealing or outright refusal to obey orders, the man would be sent ashore to be court martialed. A general court martial required a panel of officer judges, an officer prosecutor, and an officer to serve as defense lawyer for the accused. There were enough officers for that on a big ship or a shore base, but not on a PC. We also had no brig, the navy term for a jail or a place of confinement. We could send a serious offender to a brig on shore but we had no guard, personnel or space.

The main punishment practicable for us was the loss of liberty – of the chance to go ashore when we were in port. That was more serious than it sounds because there were long stretches at sea. The thirty cups of coffee a day weren't a substitute for dissipation, and many of the men lived for the day when they could go ashore and get drunk. Loss of liberty could be handed out at a "captain's mast" which was an informal procedure conducted solely by the commanding officer with the culprit required to fend for himself. Some thought Chapin dispensed too much loss of liberty. We had a few ornery and obstreperous men in the crew and I didn't feel that he had much option. Many in the crew did not respect Chapin because they had heard he was in bad with his superiors on shore. Morale was not good. Of course, part of that was due to limitations in space and PC problems: no movies, no ice cream, cramped quarters and limited fresh water.

The Hawaiian war theatre was still definitely a combat zone. The Japanese had demolished Pearl Harbor once. They were still very much on the prowl in the Pacific and there was a chance they might attack again. Submarines were a particular worry. Vigilance was crucial.

On July 17, 1943, I received a cablegram saying our baby daughter had been born that day, in Chicago. All were well. By prior agreement the baby was named Geraldine. My wife was living with her parents. The mail service was good and we kept in close touch. The mail was also kind in another way. West Publishing Company, the leading publishers of reports of court decisions, undertook to send to any lawyer in the service who requested them, the printed "advance sheet" books of all appeals court decisions in his home state. I accepted and those current reports of decisions helped to keep me up to speed on developments in Illinois law. I pored over them many an hour.

As head of four of the six departments on the ship, I had my own paper work. I joined the other officers

66

in the doubly irksome task of censoring outgoing mail of the enlisted men. It was an incredibly boring job. Even worse, it was embarrassing because the men often poured out their hearts to girl friends or to their loved ones at home. No one was supposed to say in a letter anything to indicate where our ship was located. If there was any such reference in a letter, the offending words were cut out with a pair of scissors. It was another aspect of the necessary but unrelieved lack of privacy for those serving on a navy ship.

Toward the end of the year we received orders to escort a merchant ship loaded with supplies all the way out to Tarawa which had recently been retaken from the Japanese. We knew the *PC-597* wouldn't be coming back for duty in the Hawaiian theatre of operations. Tarawa is one of a group of small, sparsely populated islands, called The Gilberts. The Gilbert Islands, which had been a British colony, straddled the equator. Tarawa was twenty-five hundred miles from Pearl Harbor, just north of the equator and west of the international dateline.

The merchant ship we were escorting could only make good a speed of 10 knots—about 12 miles per hour, less than 300 miles each 24 hours. It took us nine days and nights to make the trip. We knew Tarawa was a nothing place, certainly not an exciting destination. But, as the petty officer had said about the effect of drinking hair tonic, at least it was "different."

The trip was boring but that is true of most long stretches on a small naval ship—no movies, no ice cream, no stops along the way. We made what fresh water we could, but it wasn't enough for fresh water showers. The Hawaiian climate is the best in the world but as we went south toward the equator, the heat became worse and worse. Ensign Ryan continued to sit out shirtless in the blazing sun in accordance with his plan to try to get a medical transfer to shore duty.

We practiced the various drills. The most important one was General Quarters which meant everyone on board donned a steel helmet and a life jacket and went to his battle station. During this alert even the cooks and mess stewards had a battle station as part of a gun crew or depth charge crew. Other drills were Man Overboard and Fire and Rescue. A drill was announced over the ship's public address system and the ship's siren sounded.

A necessary activity was chipping blistered paint and repainting. Painting wasn't supposed to be done merely for the sake of appearance because paint is flammable and it was important to avoid increasing the risk of fire in case of an attack. The navy regulation was "paint to preserve only." Nonetheless you could usually tell that a ship, navy or mercantile, was poorly run if it was covered with rust spots.

We no sooner arrived at the unimpressive lagoon which made do as a harbor at Tarawa than there was a Japanese air raid. We went to General Quarters and tried to get a shot at a Japanese plane but none came low enough. We took on fuel and provisions but didn't go ashore.

We received orders to proceed to Guadalcanal in the central Solomon Islands – another twelve hundred miles of nonstop sailing. The correct word in navy language for moving forward in the water was "steaming," regardless of the kind of ship. Diesel engines such as ours, of course did not use steam.

The day after we left the Tarawa atoll we crossed the equator. There is a tradition, applicable to all kinds of ships, that crossing the equator calls for a boisterous initiation ceremony. On a civilian liner this would include people in various costumes such as ones depicting King Neptune and a retinue of mermaids. We had a few seasoned crew members who had previously crossed the equator and they took over as ringleaders of a rowdy free-for-all. Enlisted men and officers alike were doused with heavy lubricating oil and whatever other obnioxious liquids were available. The officers went along with the fun and no one wanted to pull rank to avoid a messy baptism. With very little fresh water available it took some effort later to clean up one's messy state.

It seemed to grow hotter by the day—and intensely humid. Fortunately I have never suffered from the heat—but most of the ship's complement did during the whole stretch in the South Pacific. A menace which was common was something called by the vulgar name of "foot rot." It was just that: a persistent and pervasive condition similar to athlete's foot with disgustingly soft skin between the toes. A fresh water shower was a highly desired event. We often ran through a squall with torrential rain beating down and all of us, except those on watch, stood on the open deck clad only in our undershorts and let the soaking downpour give us a shower.

Guadalcanal was an island on the south side of a limited strip of water for which the north side was another island called Tulagi. The headquarters for ships of our category was in Quanset huts on Guadal-canal. As before we received our orders by radio from shore and on only a few occasions actually went onto Guadalcanal proper. It was not a harbor – merely a beach protected by a nearby island. Tulagi was the harbor and the *PC-597* went in there and tied up, available for escort duty. The Solomons were a former British possession, not far north of Australia and were the furtherest land point south of the Japa-nese takeover of the Pacific.

The Solomons were in a transitional stage. The Americans and Australians were firmly established at Guadalcanal and Tulagi. But further west along the several hundred mile chain of islands was Bougain-ville and the Japanese troops were still there carrying on a hit-and-run guerrilla operation. The Japanese, at just about the time that the *PC-597* arrived further east at Purvis Bay by Guadalcanal, had launched a major attack on Bougainville Island with troops com-ing ashore from destroyers. One of those badly wounded in that engagement was Marine Lieutenant Orville Freeman who eighteen years later became, and still is a close friend of mine when we served to-gether in President Kennedy's cabinet. Orville, who had been governor of Minnesota, was secretary of ag-riculture. I was postmaster general.

Tulagi was a port. We put in there when we were not on assignment, which was mainly to go out sev-eral hundred miles east and rendezvous with and es-cort merchant ships bringing in supplies. The natives on the Solomons weren't far from the Stone Age. They were dwarfed and dirty, often afflicted with disease including elephantiasis – grotesquely oversized feet and hands. Our men traded with them giving canned corn beef hash from the ship for crude bead necklaces, decorated shells and grass skirts. The alleged genuine native grass skirts were in fact, in many cases, made by United States Navy enlisted men. The miserable natives acted as middlemen, and the navy men ended up with dollars paid by their unsuspecting colleagues. All this junk was mailed home to girl friends and relatives. There was no temptation for our crew to seek crude "romance" with the females of these miserable people. But there was shore liberty of sorts and plenty of beer to drink.

Australian submarine chasers would also tie up at the docks in Tulagi. Their officers carried hard liquor on board and Chapin and I spent many evenings, when not underway, on their ships, playing cards. They were boisterous and fun loving and had been in the war two years before Pearl Harbor. Australians fought and died all over the world to support the Empire. Australia today (1988) is largely independent of British control but the Queen of England is still the Queen of Australia.

Now that we had a new home port, we began receiving mail again, quantities of it, including my pamphlets of Illinois court decisions from West Publishing Company. The location of each navy ship was supposed to be secret. As I have mentioned, letters home could not tell where we were. Then how was mail to a ship like ours routed? All mail to navy ships in the Pacific was addressed to the person and the ship's name and number, care of Fleet Post Office, San Francisco. People at a mammoth mail facility there had information as to the home ports of ships and sent the mail on to us, usually by air. We were encouraged to use aerograms made of lightweight paper. "Mail call" was very important on a ship far away from home. On outgoing mail the obnoxious but necessary censoring process went on.

CHAPTER FIFTEEN

Mosquitoes and malaria were major worries in the South Pacific. A naval radio station on Guadalcanal, which broadcast news and popular music to be picked up by ships in the area, was called the Mosquito Network. Atabrin was the medication for malaria and the radio station had "The Atabrin Cocktail Hour."

On the whole it was a thoroughly unpleasant existence. The heat and humidity were, for nearly everybody except me, a twenty-four hour misery. The ship was, of course, not air conditioned and in officers' staterooms and crowded crew's quarters alike, we had no ventilation but blowers sending blasts of the hot sticky air from the open deck level.

Besides rendezvousing with and escorting merchant ships bringing supplies, fuel, and ammunition to the major base at Purvis Bay and Tulagi, we escorted ships to other islands. All of them were relatively close to Australia and we all salivated at the prospect of going into an Australian port with the American-like populace and fun. None of us were Puritans—the officers were reasonably restrained—but the members of the lower ranks of the crew craved drunkenness and willing women.

We went into one island that was Allied-occupied but otherwise primitive. Officers had come and gone assigned to the *PC-597*, but we usually had five so there were four of us to go ashore at this island. Typically our pressing priority was to find the officers' club. I have mentioned our brash ensign. We were on foot and it seemed to be quite a way to our goal. There were rutted roads of sorts. Up ahead of us a station wagon appeared with a United States Navy driver and a naval officer as a passenger. Our ensign yelled loud and clear "Hey buster, how about giving us a lift?" The station wagon waited and as we approached, "Buster" turned out to be an impressive four-striper naval aviator captain. We piled in and took off for the cherished goal. The four-striper tried to be reasonably friendly with our low-on-the-totem-pole group. Our ensign was, of course, undeterred by rank and was talkative and palsy-walsy. The captain said "Where have you boys been?" Our ensign said "We have been to Tarawa" to which the four-striper replied with limited modesty; "I took Tarawa!" It turned out we had hitched a ride with Captain Ballantine, commanding officer of the aircraft carrier *Bunker Hill*. That ship had indeed been a major participant in the bloody action to take the miserable little atoll called Tarawa. Whether Captain Ballantine had been the senior officer present, and therefore "took Tarawa" I doubt, but perhaps he was.

Navy ranks had their problems, as the above illustrates. A navy captain is the same level as a full colonel in the other services. But no one higher than a captain is ever the actual commanding officer of a ship. This is true of present day (1988) battle carriers, such as the *John F. Kennedy*, which has a complement of five thousand officers and men. The large naval vessel may indeed be the flagship of a fleet or a large squadron and carry on board rear admirals, vice admirals, or even on rare occasions a full four-star admiral. But these flag officers, as they are called, are only in charge of grand strategy or of movements of a substantial number of ships. No matter how important the flag officer (and staff) the naval ship – cruiser, carrier or battleship – may carry on board, the four-striper captain is still in charge of the ship – its navigation, its gunnery, its internal administration. Can you imagine an Army chicken colonel (so called because he wears gold eagles on his shirt collar tabs) being in charge of an army if a general (brigadier, major, lieutenant or full) was present and presiding. Another oddity – in peacetime the navy has no active duty rank comparable to the one-star brigadier general in the other services. In World War II, a rank at this level was activated – commodore – but these people were usually former captains who had been "passed over" by selection boards for advancement to rear admiral. They were always in shore assignments and never commanded or rode on ships at sea.

Captain Ballantine delivered us to the officers' club. After a few rounds of bourbon and Coca-Cola, which was the popular drink, the nothing little island began to look better.

We escorted cargo ships to the French city of Noumea in New Caledonia, a large island not far from Australia, and a major source of the valuable mined ore – nickel. Under the French colonial system, a colony, such as New Caledonia or Algeria, was a part of France and in peacetime elected delegates from these colonies sat in the parliament in Paris. Noumea was, at least, a moderately modern city and we found it a big improvement over most other ports of call, particularly the miserable, pigmy like people of the Solomon Islands.

CHAPTER SIXTEEN

We are now in early 1944. Momentous things happened in the war that year. In Europe, the Americans and British landed in January at Anzio on the west Italian coast. Italy was no longer in the war but the Germans fought hard to hold that country and it was not until June 4, that the Americans and British entered Rome.

Two days later came fateful D day—the massive movement of Allied forces across the English Channel for the invasion of Normandy. By an incredibly successful deception the Germans were duped into thinking the invasion would come further east along the coast at the shortest cross channel distance—from Dover, England to Calais, France.

In July 1944, Hitler was wounded in a bomb plot. In August, Paris was liberated and in October, Athens was freed. Late in the year when the Allies were making steady progress toward invading Germany, the Germans launched a powerful counteroffensive in Belgium—the famous "Battle of the Bulge."

In the Pacific in 1944, the Americans, with help from forces of the small populations of New Zealand and Australia, engaged in what was called "Island hopping." New Guinea was recaptured and in October, the Philippines were invaded and retaken. In early 1944, progress in the Pacific seemed discouragingly slow. Most of us continued to think it would be many years before Japan could be defeated, "Golden Gate in '48' " was still our slogan.

At home, Franklin Roosevelt was elected to a fourth term. He was showing signs of ill health but carried on without respite—the leader of the entire free world.

The *PC-597* had not been in the South Pacific long before I realized again that for some unknown reason our ship seemed to be "in bad" with the headquarters officers on shore from whom we received our orders. Our commanding officer (i.e., captain) Lieutenant Chapin seemed to be doing a satisfactory job. I never knew what was the matter—but something certainly was. Chapin was notably overdue for transfer back to the mainland for further training and assignment to a larger ship. I was disturbed by the fact that I wasn't moving up the ladder in what I then fully expected to be three or four more years of navy active duty.

I wrote a personal letter to my good friend back in Washington, Luis de Florez, by than a four-striper captain, telling him about my situation and my frustration. In only a couple of weeks an official letter came addressed to me, incredibly ordering me to proceed at once by Number Three priority travel to the Special Devices Section in Washington, D.C. I later learned that Luis had followed his frequent practice of bypassing prescribed channels. The Bureau of Navigation, which handled assignments of all naval officers, did not even know the letter to me had been sent (of course, I didn't know that at the time). Moreover, the letter should not have been sent to me but to my superiors at our ship's command center on shore at Guadalcanal. At a minimum it should have been sent to Chapin as my commanding officer.

I received the surprise orders in early April 1944. At the time the *PC-597* was at a dock in Espiritu Santo—lush, primitive islands south of the Solomons which were reputed to have cannibals in residence. The peacetime form of government of these beautiful but almost totally undeveloped islands was unusual. They were a joint, undivided colony of Britain and France, grandly called a codominium—not condominium.

The arrival of my orders caused a stir of no mean proportions on the *PC-597,* and also among the officers of other small navy ships tied up near us, and at the shore base where we picked up our mail and requisitioned fuel, spare parts, and provisions. Such orders, sent directly to the officer involved, were unprecedented so far as any of us knew.

But rather than resenting this "gift from God" that had come my way, everyone involved was quite excited and supportive. It is hard to exaggerate how desperately anxious officers and crew alike were to get away from this hot, foot-rot environment and back to the mainland. The shore base arranged the transportation details.

I flew from Espiritu Santo in a stripped down, nononsense naval personnel propeller plane for overnight in Funafuti. This was an example of the weird, nothing places dotting the Western Pacific. It had been part of a group of islands which had been a British Crown Colony. The atoll had a total area of only one square mile but a United States military base had been established there in 1943, and there were an airstrip and sleeping quarters. It was a useful stop-over point between the South Pacific and Hawaii or the West Coast. After all, there were no jets then and no planes that could fly nonstop across the Pacific. Stopping along the way for refueling was essential.

The next leg of the trip was in a naval flying boat – which could take off from and land on either land or water. These awkward looking planes were called *PBY*'s and were used extensively in the Pacific war. Our overnight stop was at Canton Island, another small atoll with an airstrip, a naval base and sleeping quarters. Before the war it had been controlled jointly by the British and Americans, and before the war and for a short time thereafter it was a refueling stop for Pan American Airlines civilian flights.

There was an overnight stop at the naval air base on the island of Oahu near Honolulu. The next leg of the trip – to San Francisco – was on a large Pan American flying boat which before the war was called the *Hawaiian Clipper*. The passenger area on this monstrosity – which had an airspeed of only 125 miles per hour – was so large it was like a flying ranch house, with several large rooms. The passengers slept in two "dormitories" – separate ones for men and women. When it was time for bed you took off your clothes, put on pajamas and got into a berth similar to one on a Pullman sleeping car. For meals you went to a dining room, and sat at one of several tables with other passengers. It all seemed unreal. There were linen tablecloths, good silverware, and food such as served in a good restaurant. The trip to San Francisco took over twenty hours. In between eating and sleeping, we sat in a large lounge reading, playing cards and dozing. A modern jet makes the trip from Hawaii to San Francisco in less than five hours.

In San Francisco, I had another stopover and then proceeded to Chicago on a regular commercial flight. My wife met me at the airport and we went to her parents house north of Chicago where I saw our baby Geraldine – by then seven months old.

CHAPTER SEVENTEEN

I reported in accordance with my orders to the Special Devices Section. I had been away from it for well over a year. During the interim, it had grown enormously. Luis de Florez was now a four-striper captain (same level as an army colonel). Since he was never shy or lacking in ingenuity, his section was no longer located down in the "temporary" buildings which were naval headquarters on Constitution Avenue. He had his own building—the former location of a large Chevrolet agency at 610 H. Street, N.E., (no non-military cars were built during World War II). The building had offices and meeting rooms and testing laboratories and the former showroom was filled with examples of naval aviation synthetic training devices used to help train naval air personnel.

Most of my old friends were there, still with the section, and there were dozens of new people. The section had tripled in size while I had been away. The whole place pulsed from the influence of Captain Luis' dynamic personality. He immediately called me into his office. He said the reason he had had me ordered back was because a close friend of his, the rear admiral who was commandant of the huge Navy Air Training Station at Pensacola, Florida, wanted a young officer for his personal aide. An aide of that sort wears a gold colored "rope" hanging from one shoulder of his uniform, moves about at the beck and call of his boss, and follows up to see that the boss's orders are being carried out. Luis and the admiral had agreed I was just the man for the assignment.

But, Luis said, a hitch had developed because I now had a "deck" classification and the aide to an air rear admiral was supposed to have an "aviation special" classification such as I had had when I was in the Special Devices Section. Luis told me it would take a little time to work things out – that in the meantime I should give some talks to the personnel of the section and become familiar with the new devices the section had developed.

My feelings about the aide assignment were mixed. It was a job for which many naval officers would have given their right arm. An aide to a rear admiral with such a key assignment as commandant at Pensacola moved in high circles, in his work and socially, and was present at important decision-making sessions. I felt just as strongly as ever that the war was going to last at least until 1948, and the aide assignment had a good chance of putting me on the fast track up the naval rank and responsibility ladder.

Military rank during the war was often a frustrating fact of life. Some highly qualified or brilliant men were taken into the armed services straight from civilian life, with no military training whatever and given the rank of colonel. George Ball, who later became undersecretary of state, was one of those. It seemed easier for a person with education to achieve high rank coming straight in from civilian life rather than starting lower down and inching up through promotions.

Commander Hibbard, still the number two officer in Special Devices, set up groups to hear me talk about my experiences. I remained in Special Devices for about two weeks, and spent some time with my wife and baby daughter.

Then another one of those unexpected things happened which impacted my naval experience in a major way. An officer could go over to the Bureau of Navigation and look at his official personnel file. I went over and looked at mine. The top item was a carbon copy of orders for me to becoming commanding officer of *PC-597*. The original had just been sent out. It became obvious to me that the Bureau of Navigation did not realize I was not present on board the *PC-597*—that I was in fact in Washington, D.C. on temporary assignment. Luis did things in wondrous ways.

I went back to Special Devices headquarters and told Luis what I had discovered. I said if it was all right with him, I would like to forget the aide to the rear admiral idea and go back to the *PC-597*. Luis accepted and I was soon on my way.

I flew back to the West Coast on a commercial propeller plane, then by the enormous *Hawaiian Clipper* back to Pearl Harbor, by naval planes for overnight stops at Canton Island and Funafuti. By chance, the *PC-597* was in Espiritu Santo again and I flew into that primitive island. With no advance notice, I stepped back aboard the *PC-597*.

No orders had arrived for Chapin or for me, and none of the officers of the ship had the slightest inkling about the change that was about to take place. They all thought by some miracle I had gotten myself ordered back to Washington so that I could bring about the change of command. There was good reason for them to think that is what happened.

Chapin was, of course, very pleased with my news because it meant he would be going back to the mainland for further training and reassignment. We had a very good third-in-line officer on board by then, Lieutenant j.g. Ford, so there was no problem about my replacement as executive officer.

CHAPTER EIGHTEEN

It was a week before the orders arrived. Chapin departed and I took over as commanding officer. An immediate change was that I, as captain, began standing deck watches the same as the other officers. Chapin had never done so.

We were very close to Australia and we all hoped to go into a port there. We had many get-togethers with Australian ships' officers and we knew they were a fun-loving lot. But no such luck. We headed north again to resume our escort duties in the vicinity of the Solomons. There were still Japanese fighting men holding out at Bougainville.

Not long after we got back to the Solomons we had a close call. It is described as follows in a book published by Pyramid Books in 1960 just before John F. Kennedy took over as president. The title was the *Kennedy War Heroes.* I was about to become Kennedy's postmaster general:

J. EDWARD DAY,
POSTMASTER GENERAL

ANY MAN'S WAR is a snail-like crawl of days, an infinity of tedium, slashed occasionally by moments of terror and action sometimes almost too swift to be recalled. Not infrequently, the fright is inspired not by the enemy, but by comrades in arms.

And so it was with J. Edward Day, a twenty-nine-year-old Chicago lawyer turned sailor, on a night in August, 1944, while he was serving as commanding officer of PC 597, a one hundred and seventy-foot steel-hull sub chaser detailed to escort duty in the Solomon Islands of the South Pacific.

PC 597 had returned to Purvis Bay, the harbor for the famed island of Guadalcanal, after escorting a liberty ship. In the harbor lay a gasoline tanker, unable to get under way because its own escort vessel was out of commission. Lieutenant Day asked the skipper of the tanker if he'd like a substitute shepherd.

He would indeed and Day got radio permission from command headquarters of the escort fleet to turn around and make another run to Bougainville, the terminal of the tanker run in that sea sector.

Day's chaser took its position 1,500 yards ahead of the tanker and the voyage began uneventfully. But about half way to Bougainville a violent tropical storm lashed the seas and brought torrents of rain cascading to the decks of the two ships. Blinded by the downpour, PC 597 picked its way by radar between treacherous reefs and shoals.

An alarm from the radar operator brought Day to the scope. There suddenly, all about them, the radar showed, was a large convoy, obviously steaming in the opposite direction. Day reduced speed and the ship groped its way forward in the eerie radio blackout.

Out of the rain and mist, almost dead on the port bow, loomed a shape that reminded some men of a huge apartment house. The helmsman threw the PC vessel hard right and an army transport liner rushed by so close that some men said an extra coat of paint on either vessel would have caused a collision and crumpled the escort ship.

Later, the crew learned that its ghost-like adversary was the former President Polk, converted for troop transport. Immediately Day ordered a round of signal flares fired to warn off the tanker behind. The gas-laden ship escaped by yards."

There is more in this article—written by Fletcher Knebel—about my later adventures in the war. That enormous army troop transport was so close that the men below decks in the mess hall could see it when looking almost straight up through a hatch. I later received a Navy Commendation Medal for offering to escort that tanker.

A ship—whether navy or otherwise—is called a "tight ship" if there is rigid discipline and unbending adherence to every detail of regulations. I consciously ran the *PC-597* below the "tight ship" category. It was partly because I realized what a miserable life the men in the crew led and how they hated it all, and no wonder: overpowering heat, no movies, no ice cream, rationed fresh water, few occasions to put into half civilized ports, no privacy, only boredom.

On our numerous trips escorting gasoline tankers we sometimes stopped along the way, pursuant to prescribed plan, and tied up alongside each other. I learned something intriguing. The tankers carried beer on board for sale to the crew at cost on a strictly controlled basis when the ship was not underway.

I adopted this plan—a limit of two cans per man per evening. No giving or selling of any to another man. It was easy to control. The men monitored it themselves, because they knew that the whole thing wasn't strictly in accordance with regulations and the beer could be cut off immediately if the restrictions weren't followed. It worked beautifully. The crew appreciated it and there was no fudging.

Another thing concerned uniforms. Everyone was supposed to wear a shirt and full length trousers at all times except during bunk time. The idea was that in case of attack and resulting fire most of the area of the body would be covered and the risk of widespread burns would be reduced. But in those runs or courses near the Solomons, we weren't likely to be attacked. It was too hot for shirts and long pants, particularly in the engine room hellhole. The men had had enough sun so that the danger of sunburn wasn't serious. Dress was allowed to be rather minimal.

One late afternoon we were "steaming" alone and were scheduled to stay the night at one of the sparsely populated Solomons, Treasury Island. A full-fledged United States destroyer was the only other ship around and it was anchored near the jungled shore. In accordance with our usual practice, and in order to make the approaching hours a little more tolerable with a movie and ice cream, we signaled by flashing light requesting permission to tie up alongside. Permission was granted.

We moved slowly and cautiously to a parallel position and the lines (ropes) went over and were secured. Our crew swarmed aboard the destroyer and mingled with the men on that much larger ship. Very soon an enlisted man from the destroyer appeared on the PC-597 and, after finding out I was captain, told me orally that the destroyer captain wanted to see me immediately in his cabin. It was a three-striper commander, presumably regular (Annapolis graduate) navy.

He barely greeted me and as though I were a lackey of some sort, proceeded to give me a severe dressing down because the *PC-597* crew was not in proper uniform: not wearing shirts and long trousers. The fact is that getting dressed up for a stop at Treasury Island would have been about like wearing a tuxedo to a pigsty. Moreover, he actually had no jurisdiction over me or our PC because he was not in our chain of command. However, there was no point in even thinking about any of that. As the famous Speaker of the House, Sam Rayburn, said years later: "If you want to get along, go along." I was like an errant schoolboy in apologizing for the nondescript appearance of the *PC-597* crew. Without making a big thing of it I had the word passed for our crew to put on the precious shirts and dungaree trousers. Some of them even shaved and combed their hair.

The destroyer commander unbent a little and after some reasonably friendly visiting I sat with him and the officers of both ships in the front rows of benches on the destroyer main deck to watch a movie and to feast on the much desired ice cream. Our crew always liked a chance to "chew the fat" with a new audience. Some of the engineering crew and the radioman from each ship had to stay at their duty stations to keep the generators going (for electricity) and to be on the alert for any possible messages – which came in code in dot and dash Morse transmission.

After that, whenever we came alongside a larger ship (except one of our gasoline tanker friends) I saw that the *PC-597* crew appeared in at least a semblance of regular navy spit and polish.

I had another incident with a regular naval destroyer captain. Our ship was coming back from an escort mission and we were proceeding up a fairly narrow channel leading to the naval docks at Tulagi. A destroyer came up behind us and was obviously impatient to get by. I turned to the left to make room but, as it happened, the destroyer turned left at the same time. Then I turned right but the destroyer also turned right. Then still again, I went left, the destroyer went left. At this point the destroyer captain sent me a smart aleck message by flashing signal light; "I do not believe there are any Japanese submarines across my bow." This could have been embarrassing but in fact it wasn't. I was doing what I believed was the correct thing and our *PC-597* crew thought the destroyer captain was a [four-letter word]. When we got tied up at a dock, I sent the destroyer captain a note of apology by messenger. After all, it was no skin off my teeth to be respectful to a senior officer even though he had been rude and wasn't my boss.

I had very little contact with regular naval officers during the war. I am sure most of them were very fine men even though some of their higher ups were a disgrace to the country by being in a laid back condition rather than a high state of alert at the time of the Japanese attack on Pearl Harbor on December 7, 1941. Regardless of all their after-the-fact excuses, their gross negligence at Pearl Harbor was unforgivable.

About the only regular naval officers with whom I had fairly regular contact during the entire war, were Radford and Doyle and Joy Hancock at the Bureau of Aeronautics during my Special Devices days. They were brilliant and dedicated people and Radford and Doyle went to the very top in the navy in key responsibilities in battle. I wish one of them could have been in charge at Pearl Harbor on December 7.

Normally the Pacific is pacific. But there in the South Pacific with weather "lows" passing through the humid atmosphere there were typhoons. We went through two in the open sea. On a narrow, relatively small ship such as a PC, one wondered how we stayed upright. The waves were gigantic and the winds and driving rain were fierce. The proper procedure was to head into the towering waves. There was no way to get from the crew's quarters to the navigation bridge except by walking along the exposed open deck. There was a real possibility someone would be washed overboard—as Jimmy Carter was, much later, hurled by a giant wave off the deck of a surfaced submarine. His incredible good fortune was that the next big wave picked him up from the open sea and deposited him back on the submarine deck. Those PCs were ruggedly built. In those violent storms we never had a crack or a leak or an engine failure.

CHAPTER NINETEEN

One incident during those months stands out as very risky for me but at the same time somewhat ludicrous. We were anchored on the edge of a deep harbor. The crew hadn't been paid for several weeks. They wanted money for cigarettes, candy and stamps. Our ship was too small to carry cash. There was a large navy supply ship, the *Dixie,* anchored in the harbor.

The *PC-597* had finally obtained a small boat which we carried aboard. Some of us chipped in our own money to buy an outboard motor. The craft wasn't a rowboat. It was even smaller with a square prow. Such a boat (called a punt) was normally used to edge along the side of a good-sized ship, so that the crew members on the punt could scrape the rust spots and paint the hull.

I assembled all the pay folders of the sixty crew members and stuffed them into my shirt pocket. Then two crew members and I boarded the little flat-bottomed punt in life jackets and headed across the choppy water for the *Dixie* with our outboard putting.

Just before we reached the steps (ladder), leading up to the decks of the *Dixie,* some vicious characters in a speedboat roared passed us and swamped our punt. We were all out in the deep water of that bay. I thrashed so violently getting onto that ladder I didn't even go down deep enough to get the pay records wet.

The ludicrous part was that one of our crew members, who was willing but dumb, decided to "rescue" the outboard motor. Incredibly, he unscrewed it from the waterfilled (but still floating) punt. It immediately sank several hundred feet to the bottom.

I went up to the finance office of the *Dixie*, received cash for the complete payroll, and the three of us went back to the *PC-597* on a decent-sized boat provided by the *Dixie*. The punt, without outboard, was retrieved later. One might ask why I was the one to go for the money. I was not only captain but I was also supply officer and headed a couple of other ship's departments as well.

Along the way a couple of officers showed how arrogant and inconsiderate some people could be. Some of the crew members were barely literate. They had to write out receipts for their cash pay. It seemed that "ninety dollars" was a common amount of pay. Invariably some of the crew, in writing out their receipts, left the "e" out of ninety. An officer who was the type who wanted to show his importance would reject the receipt as though some serious offense had taken place.

Not long after I became captain our two super lazy ensigns were moved to other assignments and we had a good, cooperative group of officers, sometimes four and sometimes five. Fortunately, they all played bridge, Acey Ducey (backgammon) and cribbage (a boring game if there ever was one.) A couple of officers and our Chief Quartermaster, Yoemans, played chess.

During long, uneventful, womanless stretches on convoy runs, some naval ships had trouble with homosexual activity among crew members. Very few of those involved were physiologically homosexual. Some did it for a break in the monotony. Some did it in the hope of being kicked out of the navy and sent home. On some ships, long away from civilized ports, the problem became a pervasive plague of epidemic proportions. For some captains it presented an unprecedented dilemma: it wasn't practical to obtain dishonorable discharges for all those men and send them home. The culprits wouldn't mind the disgrace. All they wanted was to get back stateside and enjoy their customary low-life life-style. More important, many of those men performed adequately or well at their assignments and couldn't be spared. By some unexplainable good luck, I never had the problem, although I learned later from one of the *PC-597* officers that there was an incident not long after I was transferred off the ship. Only three men were involved and they were all given dishonorable discharges.

As 1944 went on, the war in Europe was making slow but steady progress toward the defeat of Hitler. It wasn't always a sure thing. As I realized fully later, at first hand, the Germans continued to fight skillfully and ferociously to the bitter end. The Japanese would have too if it hadn't been for the atomic bomb.

We on the antisubmarine ships in the Pacific, still had not the slightest hint of development of an atomic bomb. The American and Australian-New Zealand forces continued the slow and bloody strategy of "island hopping," getting a little closer with every step to the Japanese main islands but with the inconceivable prospect of an invasion of the home base of that fanatical enemy. We still thought the war would last several more years. Even if the war in Europe ended, the British would be too exhausted by losses of men and ships – not by loss of fighting spirit – to be much of a factor in the Pacific fighting. The Soviet Union did not declare war on Japan until August 1945, after the first atomic bomb had been dropped.

Japanese submarines were a continuing threat. Late in the war they sank one of our heavy cruisers, the *Indianapolis,* with an enormous loss of American lives. Subsequent news stories of the aftermath of that cruel disaster galled me personally. The senior naval officer on the Philippines at the time of the *Indianapolis* sinking north of those islands, was a man I had met early in the war before Pearl Harbor and before I had gotten my color blindness problem straightened out. The man who introduced me to this officer had said, "Ed here is a great admirer of Franklin Roosevelt." The officer was a real Roosevelt hater. He sneered and said to me with contempt in his voice, "I admire your courage more than your judgment." I never forgot it. Later, in the course of the war, that officer received a medal of some kind, apparently presented to him by President Roosevelt. After the *Indianapolis* was sunk, charges flew that the naval command in the Philippines had failed to warn the heavy cruiser of the fact, known to that command, that Japanese submarines were operating in the area into which the *Indianapolis* was headed. The officer in question was on the spot and there was an extended investigation. The press reported – we got extensive news bulletins by radio on naval ships – that the officer actually said: "You shouldn't be investigating me for possible dereliction of duty because I was given a medal by Franklin Roosevelt." It made my stomach turn.

Unfortunately, as I will mention later, many military officers were of the right-wing persuasion. This was particularly true of regular, career officers. Thank the Lord our military establishment was then, is now, and always has been headed by civilians.

CHAPTER TWENTY

Then came the orders. I was to go back to the Submarine Chaser Training Center in Miami for further training. The orders didn't say so, but that meant being trained to go to a larger ship. The transition was easy because the executive officer, Lieutenant Ford, was such an outstanding man and was respected by the crew. He was well prepared to take over. This time there were no Priority Three urgent travel orders such as I had had when Captain de Florez had arranged to have me brought back to Washington, D.C.

This time I was sent to a carrier, along with hundreds of other naval officers, as an "officer passenger" for the long trip home by sea. It took us eighteen days to make it to San Diego. We passengers had no duties, no bosses, no access to the areas (officers' country) where the officers assigned to duty on the carrier lived, ate and slept. We were steerage. We slept on cots on the hangar deck which is next below the flight deck where the planes take off. The cots were also our place to sit during the day. We were well fed and saw movies at night. But it was the most concentrated experience of unremitting idleness I had ever experienced, before or since. The big activity was sending out our laundry which was done on machines by the ship's crew. We elected – I am not making this up – a laundry officer. He was a serious-minded person who always pronounced the first four letters of "laundry" to rhyme with "clown."

The carrier operated under a blackout and was fast enough not to need an antisubmarine escort. It was a twelve thousand mile nonstop trip.

Thank the Lord, I enjoyed playing cards. I knew three of the other officer passengers who had been on other ships that had operated in our area in the South Pacific. We four spent eighteen days playing cards together: seven-card rummy all morning and bridge all afternoon. The four of us played eighty-five rubbers of bridge during those eighteen days.

Why didn't we read or do something more constructive? There was no privacy and no room. We did our card playing sitting on the sides of cots which were in close together rows.

Sitting on the rim of a cot is hardly like sitting in an easy chair. We four played for money but we were so closely matched that the big total winner in that whole series of marathon sessions netted only twenty-five dollars.

With that long, long trip, and many more to follow, I traveled in the eight months after leaving the *PC-597* over fifty thousand miles – none of it by plane. There weren't too many nonmilitary planes in those days and non-priority people in uniform did not fly on military planes.

I mentioned at the beginning that I had a close call on getting into the navy at all because when I signed up I weighed only 131 pounds which was below the minimum. After I got to sea and experienced all the outdoor life and huge meals I soon put on 25 pounds.

I'm sure I picked up several more pounds on that carrier because in addition to the overly plentiful meals three times a day we could, and did, buy candy, snacks and ice cream to help while away the time.

It was strange being on that carrier. We were officers, some with notable combat records, and yet we had no contact whatsoever with the carrier's officers. We were only passengers. We were naval officers in limbo. Aside from the stimulus of competitive card playing, our minds were in neutral gear.

We finally arrived in San Diego harbor. I said goodbye to my three card-playing friends, to our "lowndry officer," and to some others I had gotten to know, and took a train for Chicago. It wasn't one of the faster luxury trains but I had a Pullman berth and plenty of trips to the club car and the dining car.

My wife, Mary Louise, had driven from the suburb of Winnetka into Chicago to meet me. She was in a good car belonging to her parents (in 1942 we had sold our practically new Plymouth for seven hundred dollars) but a wheel fell off the car she was driving. We finally made connections and before long I was in Winnetka seeing my little daughter, Geraldine (Jerry) only for the second time. She was seventeen months old by then.

After a brief stopover, Mary Louise, Jerry and I took a train for Miami for my second stint at Submarine Chaser Training Center (SCTC). We went back to Mrs. Morrison's, the small apartment building on Biscayne Bay where we had lived during my earlier assignment to SCTC. Mrs. Morrison had perfected still further her already considerable skill at extracting big bucks from people in uniform. The two-bedroom, two-bath apartment to which we were assigned was divided into two units with the back bedroom and bath separated from us by a shoulder-high partition. There was a light with a hanging turn off cord over the partition. We never saw the occupant of that sub-apartment in the back but on occasion an arm appeared over the partition and pulled the light cord. Jerry's crib was pushed out onto the little glassed-in porch during the evening hours when we were up and awake, and pulled back into the main room when it was time to go to bed.

Like many mid-winter visitors to Florida then and now, we deluded ourselves about the temperature which was, in fact, often definitely chilly. We went with friends over to the ocean beach on weekends and sat around on the sand with goose pimples. During that time, I met for the first time two people who are today (1988) among our most favorite friends, the Austin Kiplingers. He was in Miami Beach for advanced air force training. His father had started the famous Kiplinger Letters which our friend runs today.

The student body for our more advanced course was all officers who had had extensive sea duty. There were many classroom courses and much homework. We were being prepared for duty on destroyer escorts which were a larger class of antisubmarine ships being turned out in quantity by public and private shipyards. They were about the size of full-fledged destroyers but were slower and therefore could be built faster. They were more than fast enough to escort convoys of slow moving merchant ships and could withstand heavier seas than the much smaller PCs and SCs.

I always thanked my lucky stars that I was never

assigned to an SC. They were only 110 feet long, had a crew of twenty-four and three officers. They were wood hulled and wide for their length so that they wallowed distressingly in rough seas. Yet with their much smaller size they had to be able to do everything a PC had to do – navigate alone, man the radio and sound gear and radar round the clock when underway, be prepared to use guns and depth charges, cook three hot meals a day, keep the diesel engines maintained and operational, and all the rest. They were very similar to submarine chasers used by the United States Navy during World War I. It was a mystery to me how they functioned – with so little space and so few men. But they did function and were vital to the antisubmarine effort.

A particularly fine man that I know found great satisfaction from being an SC captain during the war. He explains it this way. Some of the crew members were barely literate. Some of the younger ones had still been pretty much tied to their mother's apron strings when they went into military service. My friend didn't baby them. But he helped them to improve their reading and writing. He was their father confessor when they heard of serious family problems back home or when they had trouble with some of their shipmates. From knowing him so long and so well I knew he was smart enough to be able to walk the fine line between excessive fraternization with the crew on one hand and being available to counsel objectively about personal matters. Unfortunately I knew very few line officers who had that knack.

CHAPTER TWENTY-ONE

A surprising high point of my second stint at SCTC occurred when all the student officers were called to an assembly, referred to as a muster, on our open-air parade ground. Without any advance notice to me or any inkling on my part of what was about to happen the captain who was Commanding Officer at SCTC called me up to the front and with appropriate remarks awarded me the Navy Commendation Medal. It was a fairly rare military decoration and was in recognition of the incident in Purvis Bay in the Solomons which I described earlier where the navy gasoline tanker was in urgent need of an escort.

Another incident at SCTC was less dignified. It was the only time in my naval life when I really should have known how to swim. One morning, our entire class was told that the drill for that day was to get experience at the exercise called "abandon ship." We were to go to the end of a long, high pier which jutted out into the water, and jump in—fully dressed. A chief petty officer was in charge. The others lined up for the jump—but not me. I told the chief, "I can't swim. If I jump down there I will drown." He was incredulous. But I was adamant. He finally told me to take off my uniform, strip down to my shorts and

T-shirt, and paddle around in a nearby swimming pool while the others did their jumping. Paddle I did.

There were new wrinkles in antisubmarine warfare and some of us were sent to the naval base at Key West, Florida to learn more about them. It mainly involved analyzing "blips" on sound (sonar) gear to try to determine whether it might be a submarine or a whale or a tightly-packed school of fish or an underwater wreck. There were many false alarms in submarine detection. The sound gear works by "sweeping" in a 360-degree circle out and around horizontally from under the ship. The impulse is a sound wave, comparable to but quite different from the light wave given out by radar. In each case, if the outgoing wave hits something solid, or even appreciably more solid than the surrounding water or air, the impulse bounces off the solid or semi-solid area or object and comes back as an echo to the transmitter. This echo shows up as a "blip" on the sonar display screen. Sometimes when the ship is operating in relatively shallow water or where there are nearby underwater coral reefs, the sonar screen presents a map-like reproduction of the surrounding area below the surface. This effect is seldom seen because submarines are unlikely to be in waters where there are reefs and the sonar projector is in those situations pulled up inside the antisubmarine vessel.

Sonar men stayed at their watches for only an hour at a time with breaks for coffee or rest because sitting with your eyes glued to that screen becomes unbearably boring and the whole mission of an escort vessel is to be alert for sound gear contacts.

If the sonar man thinks he sees something suspicious on the screen he calls the officer of the deck and together they analyze the "blip." Unless it is one of those rare situations where it is almost certainly an enemy submarine, the captain will be called and he will make the decision as to whether to sound general quarters and to start dropping depth charges and firing "mousetrap" missiles which go underwater ahead of the surface ship. If the contact seems to have a strong chance of being a sure thing, the officer of the deck makes the decision to begin the attack. At Key West, we studied many simulated blips and took an intense course in distinguishing the likely from the unlikely.

Tedious as the job of a sonarman may be, it is a sinecure compared to the nerve-wracking job of an air traffic controller at a busy airport. He has his eyes glued to a radar display showing as many as several dozen blips – all representing airborne planes. How anyone can stand that duty I don't know.

A sad piece of history has just happened (July 1988). A United States Navy cruiser has shot down an Iranian passenger plane in the Persian Gulf with 290 Iranians killed. That United States ship, the *Vincennes*, had $1 *billion* dollars worth of ultra-sophisticated radar equipment and yet it couldn't distinguish a two-seater fighter plane from a huge passenger plane. Imagine our problem in World War II, with our relatively rudimentary sound gear, trying to decide whether a blip on the screen was an enemy submarine or a tightly-packed school of fish.

That's what the training at Key West was all about. During that assignment, I went down in a submarine. It was an old "R-boat" of World War I vintage. It was still useful for training purposes. It was just as important to train United States submarine officers how to avoid and evade detection by enemy antisubmarine ships as it was to train officers in United States antisubmarine ships.

Being in the submarine was a strange experience – so quiet and without motion from wind or wave. A submarine is extremely crowded. The crew on a submarine sleeps "hot sack" which means no man has his own bunk. When he gets up to go on watch another man climbs in on the same mattress or sheets. It is no place for a person with claustrophobia. There is no chance for even a few minutes of privacy.

Some people like that kind of life. It is the ultimate of being institutionalized – never alone, never lonely, never on your own. Jimmy Carter, who graduated from the Naval Academy, was an officer on a nuclear submarine. His account of that life in one of his many books makes absorbing reading. He was a brilliant, completely honest man. He was done in by the embassy hostage crisis in Iran and by the ex-movie star. I expect history to be kind to Jimmy Carter as it has been to Harry Truman who was attacked viciously by the opposition all the time he was in office.

After I finished at Key West, there was yet another school, for training in an entirely different specialty. I was to be third officer on a destroyer escort. As the third officer I would be first lieutenant on the ship. That is not a rank – it is an assignment. The first lieutenant has responsibility for the hull of the ship. His main duty is being in charge of damage control in the event of the hull of the ship catching on fire or being hit by a shell or a torpedo. So off I went to fire-fighting school in Philadelphia.

The training involved not only a great deal of classroom work but a large amount of exciting and dangerous action. We got dressed in heavy helmets which completely covered our heads (much like a diver wears) asbestos suits, and rubber boots. In those days no one knew asbestos was dangerous. We then entered steel-walled rooms where kerosene fires were blazing, and put out the fire with foam from special pressurized cannisters or fog from fine spray nozzles on water hoses. For electrical fires only foam would do because water conducts electricity.

We got quite adept at going into these blazing infernos in small teams and getting the fire under control. The steel-walled rooms were in a building designed for the purpose at the naval yard.

After two weeks of that, I went to Boston and reported to my new ship assignment, USS *Fowler*, DE-222. The ship was named after a young naval officer who was killed in action at sea early in our participation in the war.

PART II

CHAPTER TWENTY-TWO

The *Fowler* had been commissioned in Philadelphia in mid-1944: sixteen officers and 250 enlisted men. The top three officers of the original complement had been sent to other assignments.

The new captain, whom I will call Bedford Peale, was a handsome lieutenant commander of forty-five or so, older than most officers in the antisubmarine fleet. He was from New York City cafe society and had spent a great deal of his mature life sailing on pleasure yachts. He also had no hesitancy in saying that he had been a serious fan of bathtub gin. He never drank while we were underway but during off duty time on shore he was a heavy drinker.

When he came to the ship after a serious bout with the booze and after his head had cleared, he was a joy to behold as a real seagoing man. Although he did not stand watches and did not backseat drive the officer of the deck, he spent a great deal of time on the bridge — on the outdoor "flying bridge" where the officer stood his watch in good weather and on the enclosed bridge below in poor or cold weather. Captain Peale had an uncanny interest in and knowledge of wind, waves and weather. Almost by instinct, he could tell when a rain or a blow or a storm was coming. He knew the stars and the varying shades of color in the ocean. He was a sailor *par excellance.*

The men in the crew not only respected him, they were proud of him and personally devoted to him as a man. For me, although we had entirely different backgrounds, I found him one of the most likeable men I had ever known. I was primarily a student and an enthusiast for work, including paper work. Peale was an outdoorsman, a sportsman in the best sense of the word.

The executive officer of the *Fowler* was also new. I will refer to him as Richard Burnham. He, like me, was a lieutenant, but he had never served on a fighting ship. All his experience at sea had been on hospital ships. His main deficiency was that he didn't know how to bring the *Fowler* alongside a dock. In fact, I was the only officer, other than Captain Peale, of course, who did.

Burnham was a fine, intelligent officer. In fact, the whole group of officers were quite remarkable. Many in the crew, particularly among the chiefs and other petty officers were equally outstanding. But the commissioned officers were the ones I knew best. As third officer, I was chief watch officer and assigned the hours and days of officer of the deck duty to the other officers. It could have been a problem because the officers junior to me had served on the *Fowler* since it was commissioned. But, there was no friction.

Very soon after I reported aboard, the ship got underway to be part of a group of naval ships to escort a large convoy of merchant ships across the Atlantic, through the Straits of Gibraltar, to North Africa. It was typical mid-winter Atlantic Ocean weather, cold, foggy, and rough.

We left Boston Harbor at first light and went through the Cape Cod Canal to get into the open ocean to join the other naval escort ships and the merchant ships for which we were to provide the antisubmarine protection. The ships came from various ports along the northeast coast. The Nazi collapse was only a few months away but all branches of the German military machine, including their huge fleet of U-boats with their highly experienced crews, were fighting as hard as ever right up to the bitter end.

Assembling and organizing a huge convoy was a difficult task. I had had no experience with it because, as I have said, our *PC-597* in the South Pacific never took part in escorting more than two or three ships at a time – usually only one. Merchant ships are especially vulnerable near the coast where they are proceeding to their stations on their own without escorts around them.

The other officers on the *Fowler*, except our top three, had had experience with large convoys because the assignment of the ship since it was first commissioned, was to do escort duty on the run between the United States East Coast and North Africa. A large convoy was organized into a square formation – in this case with eight ships across, and eight or nine down each row. The escort ships keep up a nonstop patrol around the edges with their sound gear working. The whole collection of ships moved very slowly for several reasons.

First, an entire convoy can proceed no faster than the slowest ship which is usually 8 knots (nine miles per hour). Most of the ships we escorted were "Liberty Ships," merchant ships of ten thousand gross tons built in large quantities on a rush, assembly line basis during World War II to handle the enormous demand for supplies for our military abroad and for civilians in allied countries. They were also needed to make up for the enormous loss of shipping tonnage to German submarines. For some reason the Japanese seldom made submarine attacks or nonmilitary cargo vessels although we never knew at any given time whether this would continue to be true. It might have been because the Pacific sea-lanes during the war were less predictable.

Another reason why convoys were so slow was because of engine trouble. If one merchant ship had to slow down to half speed the entire convoy slowed down until repairs were made. If the crippled ship couldn't resume normal speed within a few hours it was left behind but this seldom happened. Each merchant ship in a convoy carried one or two 3-inch or 40-millimeter guns and ten or twelve navy men to man them. It is remarkable how seldom a ship completely loses power for its propellers as the *QE II* did several years ago near Bermuda. In that highly publicized debacle, that elegant ship had to be towed into port for repairs.

An important third reason why convoys were slow was because the entire formation followed a prescribed zigzag pattern taken from a highly confidential naval publication which described many such patterns. Each ship in the convoy was told by coded message from the naval ship carrying the most senior naval officer the number of the zigzag pattern that was to be used. The patterns required changes, of course, of as much as twenty or thirty degrees for a prescribed length of time. The idea was that an enemy submarine in the area which was tracking the convoy from underwater, wouldn't be able to make the course changes fast enough with its slow sub-merged speed, to get into a position to fire a torpedo at a merchant ship. The carnage from U-boats hitting ships bound for Britain early in the war was reduced dramatically by a widespread shift to the convoy system. That is why Britain desperately needed those fifty World War I United States "four stacker" de-stroyers President Roosevelt transferred to them be-fore the United States got into the war in exchange for naval bases for the United States on various British possessions.

Another aspect of a convoy was that the most sen-ior merchant marine captain on all of the merchant ships was the "Commodore of the Convoy." He was the boss. After radio or flashing signal light consulta-tion with the naval S.O.P. (senior officer present; also in other contexts "standard operating procedures"), the commodore of the convoy made such difficult de-cisions as to when to slow the entire formation be-cause one ship was having engine trouble, when to leave a disabled ship behind on its own, and when to change course in a way which overrode the zigzag pattern if, for example, there had been a report of a submarine contact from a convoy quite a distance ahead or from a ship or plane. Considering what a key role navy planes and helicopters play today in sub-marine detection and antisubmarine warfare, by tow-ing sound gear in the water from low altitudes, it is hard to believe that this strategy had not been developed during World War II. Even if it had, a low-flying naval, slow speed plane, let alone a helicopter, wouldn't have been much help in the middle of the foggy and stormy Atlantic Ocean in the winter months.

Where the United States got all the experienced Merchant Marine officers for all the new Liberty ships and Victory ships and merchant tankers rushed to completion during World War II is a mystery. Because before the war, and again today, the United States merchant shipping industry was very sick indeed due to huge wage differentials for crew members compared to foreign flagged ships. Today (1988), we don't read about or see television news clips about, genuine United States flagged tankers in the Persian Gulf mare's rest.

From all the above, one might wonder how these huge convoys ever got into formation and ever got to their destination. But they did and with notable effectiveness.

We were on our way across the Atlantic. Captain Peale performed his part of the job with skill and team-play reliability. The naval escort ships not only followed in general the prescribed zigzag plan but they pursued additional change of course maneuvers in an effort to "cover" with sound gear the entire circumference of the convoy. In effect they were zigzagging beyond the zigzag plan, each in a designated sector so as not to get too close to the next naval ship. The result of this procedure was that we necessarily deviated from one of the most rudimentary rules of seamanship—when the waves are mountainous, head the ship into the waves and don't get caught broadside in the trough (deep part) of a wave.

As we made our rocky way in the indescribably miserable weather, we passed Bermuda which was nothing but a blurry bit of land seen through the fog. Not long afterward, we came into a storm of terrifying force. The wind was of gale velocity, the rain came down in sheets, and the visability was close to zero. Even with radar equipment, an officer of the deck likes to see where he is going – or to have the ship's lookouts, clad in foul weather gear, and standing on the open deck, see what is ahead.

Soon after the storm broke, the lookouts had to be ordered away from their positions on deck because huge walls of water broke over the bow of the ship and not only inundated the open decks but pounded against the glass of the bridge and washed completely over the bridge. I was officer of the deck with Captain Peale with me sitting in a chair which was attached to the bulkhead of the bridge or wheelhouse. As we turned as part of our search pattern into the trough of the huge waves, the ship's instruments registered a "list" or deviation from an upright position of forty-four degrees. Each time the ship rolled over to that extreme angle one wondered if it was going to go all the way and turn over completely or whether it would somehow come back to an upright position. A 90-degree list would mean the ship was helpless on its side in the water – and we were half way there.

When we turned into the oncoming towers of waves, the "pitch" or up and down rocking motion was equally extreme. Everyone on the bridge, or in a standing position anywhere on the ship, had to cling

117

with all the strength possible to some part of the ship's structure or be thrown to the deck.

The havoc that violent movement like that creates on a ship is beyond belief. Despite all the previous orders to batten everything down, furniture was thrown around, stores fell from their shelves, the galleys and pantries were left in chaos. With those walls of water crashing over, it is a wonder we didn't lose some of our depth charges which were fastened with cables to the afterdeck.

CHAPTER
TWENTY-THREE

We made it through that storm and a couple of lesser ones that hit our convoy on that trip. One wondered how the small, frail sailing ships, with sails furled, ever made it across that cruel ocean three and four centuries earlier.

With sixteen officers, fourteen of them available to stand deck watches, each officer had fewer watches to stand, in contrast to three for each officer every forty-eight hours on the PC. Also, in my case, I had a much lighter work load at sea than I was used to. I was no longer captain, navigator, engineering officer, communications officer and supply officer as I had been during my tour of duty on the PC.

All the officers ate at one big oval table in the ward room. When the sea was rough there were "fiddle boards" or wooden walls around the table, and heavily dampened tablecloths to keep the dishes from sliding off.

After dinner and after the mess stewards had cleaned the table and put on a green felt cloth, the games began. The favorite game demonstrated the sophistication and alert minds of this group of officers. I wouldn't say they were intellectuals exactly. Most of them were ultraconservative politically and idealogically. But they were a smart bunch.

This favorite pastime was dividing into two teams and trying to stump the rival team with quiz questions. Usually each team made up its own questions – on any subject in history, sports, movies, geography and anything else. By general agreement we stuck to questions to which a well-informed person might be expected to know the answers. There were no way out questions such as "what was the name of John Wilkes Booth's horse?"

Our engineering officer, Lieutenant Reynolds, was particularly adept at these contests. He not only headed one of the teams but also was accepted by both sides as referee and moderator.

We had an old *Ask Me Another* book, a very popular publication which was published ten or fifteen years before the war. This was a gold mine of questions, particularly since we decided any question had to be given the answer which dated from the late 1920s when the book was published.

For example, the answer to the question, "What is the tallest building in the world?" was not the Empire State Building but the Woolworth Building. The answer for the capital of Australia was not Canberra but Melbourne. There were others.

Lieutenant j.g. Schussmann was also a star at this game. He was the communications officer and from his civilian background as a high school teacher, he knew a great deal about sports and music and was well-informed in general. These officers were a compatible group.

As we rocked across the Atlantic with this slow

convoy, I got started on writing a novel. I have to tell the whole story in one place about the piece of literature although the most important incident happened fifteen years after the war was over.

I wrote it all by longhand during the otherwise inactive hours, which were numerous. I had read some novels by John P. Marquand who was popular at that time. His books were similar in content to those of F. Scott Fitzgerald dealing in a mildly satirical manner with the doings of the affluent "high society" set. John O'Hara was another popular writer on that theme. To disguise the fact that much of my story hinted at recollections of my hometown of Springfield, Illinois where I had grown up and where my parents lived, I made the locale Philadelphia. I named the novel *Bartholf Street* purely by random choice. There was a prominent Springfield family with that name. I knew very little about that family so the story wasn't based on them or their activities. Only much later did one of them tell me the name was unique and so far as they knew there was no Bartholf family anywhere else in the United States.

When we came into port from time to time, I mailed the long-hand pages I had finished to my mother in Springfield. She made a typed copy. There was nothing in the manuscript which was risqué. My mother was definitely straightlaced. The leading character, a medical doctor, tried to have an affair with his sister-in-law, but she wasn't interested. This doctor was somewhat of a womanizer and the nearest to anything explicit in the sex department was that I mentioned at one point that one of his girl friends in his bachelor days appeared in her negligée.

After the war, the book was published. Time marched on and it was forgotten. Then in late 1960, I was designated by President Kennedy to be his postmaster general, at that time a full-fledged cabinet post. In those days the post office was heavily involved with pornography – trying to prevent smut from being carried in the mail. After my appointment was announced, someone dug up a copy of *Bartholf Street.* The people at the Republican National Committee were trying to find fault with President Kennedy's cabinet appointees. The chairman of that committee, a birdbrain named Miller (who ran for vice-president on the ticket with Goldwater in 1984) came out with a blast saying that Day, who was supposed to protect the public from pornography, had written a dirty novel.

I had plenty of fun with that ridiculous accusation. I told the press about how the novel had been typed by my mother. Some of them got hold of a copy (which I am sure Miller had never done) and reported that the text was as clean as a Sunday school pamphlet.

So much for Miller, that great congressman and statesman from Niagara Falls, New York. Many years later he appeared on television commercials for dog food or paint or some product. His identification on those ads was "The man nobody knows." How true.

Writing the novel did in fact occupy many idle hours during my often boring tour of duty on the DE-222. I used to read a part I had finished to other officers and they gave me suggestions as to how it could be improved. It was a satisfying group activity.

CHAPTER
TWENTY-FOUR

As the *Fowler* approached the Strait of Gibraltar, we received radio warnings of German submarines in the area. It was February 17, 1945, only three months before the Nazi surrender, but all branches of Hitler's armed forces continued the fighting with fanatical frenzy. The Gibraltar waters were a good place for enemy submarines because many huge United States convoys, bringing supplies for the fighting in Europe, had to funnel into a narrow sea-lane. On the basis of the warnings, we went to General Quarters, the state of highest battle alert.

It turned out to be twenty-four hours before that alert was over. Suddenly it happened. First one and then another of the merchant ships in the convoy were hit with torpedos in close succession. Both were disabled, dead in the water, unable to move. The senior naval officer told the convoy to continue its slow way toward the Strait and ordered the *Fowler* and another DE each to stand by in the vicinity of one of the badly damaged freighters and provide a sound gear patrol.

We kept that up for hours waiting for tugs to come out from Gibraltar and take the two ships in tow. We expected another attack, probably on the same disabled freighters, because lying dead in the winter, they were sitting ducks. Eventually the tugs arrived and the merchant ships got lines over to them and the slow tow began. We provided a screen for tugs and freighters while they crawled slowly into the comparative safety of the Gibraltar harbor. There was a huge submarine net completely across the Strait during the war and very few German submarines made it through, but some did.

I had seen the famous rock once before. In the summer of 1932, after I had finished high school in Springfield, my mother and brother and I took an escorted tour of twelve countries (price $650 each including round trip across the Atlantic on ocean liners). Gibraltar was our first stop. The evening after we left there was the first time I became inebriated. Most of our group were college-age people and some of us had gotten together costumes and put on a humorous play for the entertainment of the passengers. When it was over, the captain treated us to champagne. I had never had any before (I was still seventeen) and I drank it like soda pop. The next morning I had a monumental headache but my mother didn't want me to miss anything so she got me going with a dose of ammonia.

Back to the *Fowler*. After we left the disabled freighters at Gibraltar, we and the other DE speeded up and caught up with the convoy. The long stretch at General Quarters was finally over. While it was on, there was no hot food because the cooks were at battle stations too. Some of them were relieved of their battle assignments long enough to make sandwiches

124

and coffee and to bring these around to the ships personnel at their stations.

The strain and tension reminded me of the 15-hour hurricane my family had endured in 1926, when I was about to be thirteen years old and we had just moved to Miami, Florida. It was the worst hurricane ever, before or since, in Florida history.

With the alert over, those men that could, headed for their bunks. Some had to resume normal watches. Captain Peale didn't seem to miss sleep. He was on the bridge the whole time.

In twenty-four hours we entered the harbor at Oran, the second largest city in Algiers. For many years before the war and for a few years afterward, Algiers was governmentally a part of France with elected delegates sitting in the parliament in Paris. Large numbers of French people lived for generations in Algiers. The Germans had been driven out of North Africa long before. But Algiers was still in a near-starvation condition. Bread was rationed. Shops and stores were closed and there was little traffic on the streets.

The *Fowler* had been to Oran before and our officers and crew had a well-organized plan for obtaining some lively recreation in the impoverished city. Some of the savvy ones went ashore and rented a large vacant single floor store for the next night and hired a local orchestra. Handmade signs were posted at strategic points near the center of the city inviting young ladies to come to a dance, with refreshments furnished, the next night at the location given.

Typical of the navy, we had vast stores of provisions on board. The next day the cooks made up hundreds of turkey and ham sandwiches, gallons of potato salad, and quantities of cakes and cookies and doughnuts, all packed in large boxes.

The French people in the local population were familiar with this system. At the appointed time a hundred or more French girls, some quite attractive and all appearing to be respectable, arrived, each with her mother. Girls and mothers alike each carried a large cloth or knitted bag. The boxes of food were kept closed and out of sight. Some of our eager beavers had brought in supplies of cognac and wine and plastic cups. The mothers seated themselves stolidly around the dance floor to keep an eye on their daughters.

Most of the guests didn't speak English but the girls knew how to dance American-style. The orchestra threw themselves into playing lively American tunes. For nearly three hours, with a few breaks, the men, officers and crew alike, all washed and shaved and dressed up to do some drinking, the party went on. Even without a common language there were attempts to communicate, and much singing and laughing.

Then came the grand climax: the event the women had come for. The boxes of food were opened. As if on cue, the mothers rushed forward like a huge swarm of heavy-set locusts. The sandwiches and pastry were snatched up and pushed into the voluminous bags. Very soon, the food was gone and mothers and daughters disappeared *en masse* into the night. It all happened in minutes. Not a crumb was left. But there was plenty of cognac and the partying continued—without benefit of female companionship. Some non-drinkers put the place back in shape and paid off the orchestra. Groups of officers and other groups of enlisted men drifted off to local bars. There were taxis and busses and eventually, much later, we all made it back to the ship.

Oran was a fairly satisfactory port of call. We stayed over to wait for the merchant ships to unload so that we could escort them back across the ocean. There was a wide, sunny beach on the Mediterranean. There was a casbah, a crowded Arab slum with narrow dirty alleyways, sinister looking inhabitants, and a variety of unattractive sights and smells. Everyone asked for a handout or wanted to sell us something and there was the usual haggling over the price and not much worth buying. There were prostitutes who exhibited their charms in a blatant fashion. We took taxis and bus trips to the environs and got acquainted with officers from other naval ships. Two of us from the *Fowler* who were enthusiastic card players took up a challenge by two officers from another DE and went back on shipboard for a bridge game at a penny a point. That was pretty wild for those days. We drew a small crowd of spectators and fortunately we, from the *Fowler,* won. We went back to the ship for meals because they were good and plentiful and the few cafes that were open had little to offer. Goat meat was the big specialty. Actually meat of a young goat is quite good, about the same as spring lamb.

Much of the cargo we had brought was food and medicine and spare parts for the population of North Africa whose economy had been ground to a standstill. Also a large part of what we and other United States convoys brought was transshipped to Italy and France.

A short time before we arrived in Oran, the Yalta Conference had taken place in the Soviet Crimea. At that historic meeting, Franklin Roosevelt, who had just begun his fourth term as president, Churchill and Stalin, discussed the coming occupation of Germany and the future of the liberated people. They agreed to disarm Germany forever. The fanactical refusal of the Nazis to admit they were beaten led to a series of disasters for the Germans. The Hitler pattern was to hold ground to the last. The German army fought west of the Rhine instead of withdrawing behind it. They permitted two armies to be trapped in the triangle between the Saar and the Moselle, and thus opened a gap into the heart of Germany which they no longer had reserves to fill. They made a desperate defense of the Ruhr and allowed a huge army group to be encircled there.

They flung a series of counterattacks against the Russians in reckless attempts to relieve the 49-day siege of Budapest. These futile efforts were made at the price of being unable to withdraw to the much-touted "last stand" in the mountains of southern Germany. The vise of the Allied armies in the west and the Russian armies in the east was moving towards snapping shut on the remains of Nazi Germany. Finally, in April of 1945, the French puppet government of General Petain surrendered to the Allies.

In the Pacific it was still hard going. On January 9, General Douglas MacArthur landed a large invasion force on Luzon in the Philippines. In February, United States Marines landed on Iwo Jima, "the toughest Pacific Island" and after a 26-day assault the island fell. From newly captured Saipan and Tinian

American B-29s began incendiary raids on Japan, and their bombs pounded Japan's industrial centers. It was still uncertain when and whether Japan would give up. The ordinary citizen in and out of the uniform knew nothing about the newly perfected atomic bomb, and the prospect of massive slaughter of American servicemen from a surface invasion of the Japanese main islands still loomed. To rank and file people like myself final victory seemed a long way off.

In Oran, the merchant ships were finally unloaded, the convoy assembled, and the escort ships took their stations. The whole awkward assemblage of ships made its way back through the Strait of Gibraltar. Two days out of Oran, on February 28, 1945, I was officer of the deck when we picked up an ominous contact on the sound gear. Captain Peale was on the bridge and ordered General Quarters. We made a series of urgent depth charge attacks which brought debris to the surface. In coordination with a Free French ship we made a final attack which sank a German submarine, identified much later from German records as *U-869*.

The convoy and escorts completed the trip across the Atlantic without incident. We left the merchant ships at Norfolk and proceeded to New York harbor where we tied up at the Brooklyn Navy Yard, waiting for the next convoy assignment.

There were much chipping of rust and painting and maintenance work on the hull and the engines. We took on fuel, provisions and supplies of all kinds. And there was plenty of time for fun and games. Coming into an East Coast port for liberty had been the fond dream of the officers and crew of the *PC-597* and of

129

hundreds of other navy ships at remote locations in the far away Pacific. New York City was even more lively than usual. Victory was in the air. Everyone had a job; everyone had money. Hotels, bars, night-clubs, theatres and juke joints reflected an atmosphere of excitement.

We didn't know when our next assignment would begin so we couldn't travel any distance. But Mary Louise came from Winnetka, Illinois for a visit. Some of our officers and men had a wild time.

We weren't at sea or about to get underway so our captain, for whom New York City was hometown, went ashore and pursued his favorite hobby which was intake of gin. He came back to the ship one night pretty much under the influence. Soon after he came aboard, he learned that one of the crew members had reported that his watch was stolen. The captain ordered the entire crew to muster on deck. That meant getting into uniform and standing in long lines on the open deck. No enlisted man, not even chief petty officers, was excused.

The captain appeared in front of the assemblage and announced in a loud, clear voice that everyone was going to keep standing there until someone owned up to having stolen the watch. Men returning from liberty, joined the group with expressions of disbelief. Several times the captain repeated his announcement. He had a "bull horn" which amplified his voice electronically. For quite a while he showed no sign of relenting.

We other officers just stood around as observers. There was nothing we could do. And there was no need to do anything because we knew and the crew knew that it was John Barleycorn talking. No damage was being done because the members of the crew had such affection for Captain Peale that they did not resent the unorthodox use of authority. They were indulgent. It wasn't even close to a Captain Queeg scene from *The Caine Mutiny.* Of course no one spoke up to say he had taken the watch.

Eventually the captain, without dismissing the men, went quietly — handsome, dignified and loaded — to his cabin. The crew drifted back to their bunks or their card games or to watch a movie. No harm was done. But it was a memorable example of the respect that can be developed from the crew by a captain who was every inch a sailor.

On March 31, we got underway for the *Fowler's* sixth convoy trip to North Africa. It was another enormous assemblage of Liberty ships, Victory ships, older merchant ships and tankers. It was a repeat of the complicated job of getting the ships in the convoy into position and moving in formation. It was another long, slow trip, rough seas but not quite as bad as the 44-degree roll on the previous time out.

On the way across, on April 12, our ship received the message that President Roosevelt had died at Warm Springs, Georgia, and that Harry Truman had become president. It was not unexpected. Roosevelt had looked terrible during the 1944 campaign and in the pictures from the Yalta Conference. It was fortunate that he had dumped Henry Wallace as his vice-president and had selected the tough-minded, decisive Truman as his running mate. Wallace was a brilliant man but was too much identified with the super-liberal wing of the Democratic Party. He worried middle-of-the-road, business-oriented Democrats like me.

It was obviously appropriate to have some kind of a memorial service. Nearly all of the other officers were conservative Republicans, some died-in-the-wool Roosevelt haters. I was the obvious one to conduct the service.

Most of the members of the crew who were not on watch assembled in the largest mess hall. Some of the officers came. I read a couple of familiar psalms, gave an extemporaneous talk reviewing FDR's great accomplishments and closed by having everyone sing "God Bless America."

I felt sad about Roosevelt's death. I had admired him and defended him since he first ran for president in the fall of 1932 just as I was starting to college at the University of Chicago. During all those intervening years, ugly hatred of FDR had been an obsession with many of my social friends, with many of the attorneys in the law firm and with many fellow navy officers. His policies of borrowing and spending, which in my opinion saved the capitalistic system in the western world, were attacked viciously and unrelentingly by many as making him a "traitor to his class." The "class" wouldn't have lasted if nothing had been done for the sixteen million unemployed except to wait for prosperity to round the corner.

We made it through the Strait without incident and again tied up at the dock in Oran. There was another lively dance with the French girls in a vacant store building with the boxes of food from the ship's galley and the mamas grabbing everything within reach and filling their gaping string bags. It was just as much fun as before and there was just as much cognac. Spring had come to North Africa and the wide beaches were inviting. The casbah was just as smelley and sinister. There were more bus and taxi trips to the surrounding areas.

We rounded up the unloaded ships of the convoy and started home May 2, the day that Berlin fell. Three days after we got through the Strait, Germany surrendered unconditionally in the wee hours of the morning of May 7. There were shouts and cheers and laughter on board.

We maintained our escort positions and kept the sound gear going in case some fanatical U-boat commander decided to get off one last torpedo. It seemed more likely that one or more U-boats would surface and surrender as we made our slow way back across the Atlantic. We speculated as to what we would do if that happened. What would we do with the German crew? What would we do with the German submarine? Would we scatter the crew among our naval ships or our merchant ships? Would we put the United States Navy men aboard the submarine to be sure the German crew stayed on course for a United States port?

It was all idle speculation — because no U-boat surfaced along our path. I never heard one instance of a U-boat surrendering in the open sea during that time after the collapse of the Nazis. Presumably they all held back enough fuel to make it home to their heavily bombed submarine pens (that is what they were called) at Bremen or Hamburg. That way they might avoid becoming prisoners of war and might fade into the defeated civilian population.

The weather was better. The waves were less mountainous. We left the convoy merchant ships at Norfolk, separated from the other naval escort vessels and – pursuant to orders – headed for the Brooklyn Navy Yard.

I have no criticism of the navy as an institution, as it was then. But the next forty-eight hours, following orders from our shore command, were ludicrous. It was early evening. We came in parallel to Long Island, maneuvered through all the seagoing traffic, made the passage through "the Narrows" – the entrance to New York Harbor – and passed the Statue of Liberty. When we were within sight of the Brooklyn Bridge new orders came: reverse course and proceed to Boston Navy Yard. We turned around and went back through the Narrows and along the busy sea-lane within sight of the lights of Long Island.

We got clear to the end of Long Island, steaming toward Boston, when new orders came again: reverse course and proceed to Brooklyn Navy Yard. We radioed back to see if there had been a mistake or whether we were receiving a superceded message. The orders to turn around were confirmed. It seemed the great brains in the command center didn't know what to do with us. Or perhaps some of their officers had been overdoing it in celebrating the Germans surrender.

Back we went: Long Island lights, Narrows, Statue of Liberty, and this time *under* the Brooklyn Bridge. We were moving slowly toward the dock, at "special sea detail" which meant the crew was ready to throw the lines over and to place the bumpers (large padded elongated cushions) so that the ship would not scrape on the dock. Then, when we were within fifty feet of the dock, barely moving, it happened again. Proceed to Boston. That really happened. The men on the dock must have thought we had lost our minds. We thought somebody had. It didn't seem possible.

We pulled back into the channel and headed out again— expecting at any minute to receive still another countermanding order. But that time we finally made it. In twenty-four hours we crept into the great naval yard at Boston and actually got tied up at a dock with gangway over, fresh water connected, and messengers sent for the mail.

None of us thought that our war service was over. The Pacific war was still going full blast and each of us expected to be part of that.

We took on fuel and provisions and the shore liberty began. In a few days our feeling that no one knew what to do with us was confirmed. We were ordered to the naval base on Casco Bay, Maine. It was nearly the end of May then. Again we tied up at a dock – this time at the Naval Fuel Annex. We were supposed to operate with United States submarines to give both them and us training in antisubmarine warfare. We had barely gotten started on that, when we received orders to proceed to the naval yard at Philadelphia. For some reason those orders were on a rush basis and had to be carried out without delay.

Casco Bay wasn't a big place and it was early morning, but men had to be sent ashore to find Captain Peale who was pursuing his hobby. When he came back to the ship he was pretty bad. We couldn't delay until he had a chance to sober up because we were to make the trip with two other DEs, the *Robinson,* DE

200, and the *Solar,* DE 221. The senior officer present afloat (SOPA) was on the *Robinson.*

It took some doing to get away from the dock, through the submarine nets, out of the bay and into column formation. The officer of the deck was Lieutenant W. W. Scott, a fine, reliable officer who had been a Morman missionary and who had an appetite as voracious as mine. He loved huge meatloaf sandwiches in between meals. The executive and I assisted. Peale had gone to his cabin which was just as well because if he had stayed on the bridge he would have been in the way. Under naval practice, the commanding officer always took charge when a ship was docking at a pier or leaving a pier. Peale didn't tell us to take over. We had to. We knew what to do and we did it.

In midafternoon, after resuming a normal watch schedule, we received radio reports that a naval plane had ditched in the area ahead of us. I took over as officer of the deck at 1600 (4 p.m.) and soon thereafter we sighted a rubber life raft with a man on board. We maneuvered to pick him up. The survivor was a lieutenant (j.g.) who had been flying out of Groton, Connecticut. Our medical officer reported he was in good condition; suffering slightly from shock. The Solar picked up the other survivor. In a few hours we received radioed orders to proceed to Newport, Rhode Island, to discharge our passenger.

Our orders to Philadelphia were superseded and we went to New London, Connecticut, to engage in joint exercises with submarines. That took most of June and July and then we were ordered back to Boston. We were to be converted, by a major remodeling job, to an APD. That was a ship, not for antisubmarine duty, but for landing troops as part of an invasion force. APDs went in close to an enemy island and the marines or army men on board headed for the beach in small landing craft.

The conversion was to be a time-consuming process. The exec stayed on board in charge and most of the officers and men were given substantial periods of leave and went home. I had thirty days. Mary Louise and little Jerry were with Mary Louise's family at a vacation spot called Lakeside, Michigan, seventy miles around the end of Lake Michigan from Chicago.

I went into Boston and took a train for Gary, Indiana, the nearest station to Lakeside. In a sit-up, non-Pullman car, I jolted along for sixteen hours. I had barely gotten settled at Lakeside and into civilian clothes when a telegram arrived from the exec of the *Fowler:* "Orders for you have arrived; return to the ship at once." Why didn't he say he was mailing the orders? I never knew.

Back onto the sit-up railway car and another sixteen hours to Boston. Taxi out to the naval yard and to the ship which was in a definitely dormant state with few of the officers or crew on hand.

The letter from the Bureau of Personnel in Washington said I was ordered to San Francisco to await transportation to Guam where I was to be executive officer of a DE based there. The orders said I was granted twenty-seven days delay in reporting to San Francisco. That was a usual way of allowing extended leave to an officer who had had a considerable period of sea duty. Naturally, there was nothing in my orders about my replacement as First Lieutenant on the *Fowler.* Captain Peale had gone off to New York and I was sorry not to be able to say good-bye to him and to tell him how much I appreciated our friendly relationship as fellow officers.

I packed up all the rest of my gear, said my farewells, and got back onto a sit-up railway car for another 16-hour trip to Gary and Lakeside. Some of our friends at Lakeside wondered what was going on — and with good reason. But there was more of the same to come.

At Lakeside in August, one felt isolated and apart from the troubled big world. What with golf, tennis, the beach, and family and partying, I didn't pay close enough attention, as it turned out, to what was happening in the war. I was acutely aware, of course, of the dropping of first one, and then a second atomic bomb on Japanese cities. I knew the Japanese gave up and agreed to surrender. But I didn't focus on what this meant to me personally. I knew that, war or no war, the navy had to keep functioning. The ships couldn't be left standing at the docks unattended. The big thing I had no way to know, since I wasn't in touch with a naval ship or installation, was that soon after V-J Day (Victory in Japan) the navy had announced that reserve officers who would by September 15, 1945, have a given number of "points," should report to their home naval base and await release from military service.

"Points" were determined by the number of months of active duty with extra points for combat duty. My home naval base was Great Lakes Naval Station at Waukegan, Illinois, north of Chicago.

As the end of my 27-day delay approached, I took the train into Chicago and boarded a train for San

Francisco. Naturally the train had barely left the station when I made my way to the club car and began getting acquainted with other naval officers who were making the same trip. We, of course, began telling each other about our past service and experiences and about our next assignment. We were scarcely out of the Chicago suburbs when one of my new drinking companions said to me: "You shouldn't be on this train. With the points you have you should be heading for Great Lakes to be released from the Navy."

I couldn't very well just get off the train at some way station. I had orders to go to San Francisco and to Guam and I had no official word that changed those orders. The officers in the club car could have been wrong. So I made the long, tiresome trip across two-thirds of the United States in a non-air-conditioned railroad train. I finished writing the manuscript for *Bartholf Street*.

When I arrived in San Francisco and reported in accordance with my orders I was told officially, with necessary railway tickets supplied, to return to Great Lakes.

It is hard to exaggerate how fortunate I was that I didn't actually go to Guam. If I had, the captain of the DE to which I was to report would, in all probability, have had as many or more points than I had. He would have headed back to the mainland, and I would have taken over as captain with the duty of bringing the ship back to a West Coast port. The DE might even have been assigned duties for a number of months in the Far Pacific. If it had come back to San Diego or Seattle it might have gone through a laborious decommissioning procedure preparing it to join the mothball fleet; tied up in a cove somewhere, rusting and waiting for the next war. Decommissioning involved major paper work: making a detailed inventory of everything on board from navigation instruments and engine room tools to knives and forks in the officers' ward room.

After the war, there was a great surplusage of DEs. There wasn't a need for many of them in the peacetime navy. Some of them were kept on active status for a year or more after the war. The *Fowler,* for example, went to Miami, Florida, to serve as a school ship for the Naval Training Center. After that, she served as a plane guard (to rescue plane crews in trouble) for the aircraft carrier *Charger.* Still later, she arrived at Green Cove Springs, Florida, then and now, a major mothballing location. It was five months later before the decommissioning was complete and the *Fowler* officers and crew were sent to new assignments or released from active duty.

A number of DEs were given to South American countries. World War II United States DEs can still be seen, as I have seen them, at ports used by the navies of Venezuela, Peru and Chile. Like a DC-3 a steel-hulled ship can be kept in operation as long as maintenance is thorough.

So it was fortunate for me I didn't get to Guam. I came back to Chicago on the hot train. We went through a long tunnel with the windows open and came out covered with soot from the coal-fired steam engine.

I reported to Great Lakes. Since I was still on active duty, the navy gave me an assignment. Thousands of enlisted men were being released and the navy was providing them with transportation home. I was put in an office where, by means of Teletypes, we matched available train space from specific starting points to specific destinations with numbers of men waiting to make that trip. Even in the short two weeks I was in this hum drum assignment, it became painfully repetitious and monotonous. I applied myself to simplifying and speeding up the procedure. But I realized vividly that I was never cut out for unvarying, repetitious activity. I had never been subjected to it before and hoped never to be again.

My brother-in-law, Kenneth Burgess, was also at Great Lakes, with more than enough points, waiting for the magic date when release from active duty in the navy would happen. He had no assigned duties so he spent his time finding out every detail of the release procedures—greasing the skids, so to speak.

On the final day, we had to check out at the laundry, at the infirmary, at the library, at the records office, and at the finance office. Thanks to all his advance scouting, the two of us must have set a speed record on getting out. It was about noon on a Saturday when we finished up. I started back to work at the Chicago law office the following Monday.

Thus, five years and six weeks after I had first enlisted, I ended my career in the navy.